Rebuilding Democracy:

Strategies for Countering Political Extremism

by Thomas T. Taylor

Formatted, Converted, and Distributed by eBookIt.com
http://www.eBookIt.com

ISBN-13: (hardcover)
ISBN-13: 978-1-4566-4096-5 (paperback)
ISBN-13: 978-1-4566-4095-8 (ebook)
ISBN-13: 978-1-4566-4097-2 (audiobook)

Dear Esteemed Reader,

Thank you immensely for choosing this book to join your collection. We imagine that you've already embarked on an exploration of ideas within these pages, and we couldn't be happier about it!

Now, if you find yourself chuckling, pondering, or even debating with the words in front of you, we'd absolutely love to hear about it. If you can spare a few moments to pen down your thoughts in a review, we would be as delighted as a dictionary on a spelling bee!

An Amazon review would be excellent - but hey, we're far from picky. Whether it's a scribble on the back of a grocery list, a tweet, or even a message in a bottle (though that might take a while to reach us), your feedback is gold.

Writing a review might not be as fun as a spontaneous dance-off, but we promise it'll bring grins to our faces, warmth to our hearts, and incredibly valuable insights to future readers.

With Gratitude,

Bo Bennett, PhD
Publisher
Archieboy Holdings, LLC.

Table of Contents

Introduction..6

Promote Media Literacy 8

Engage in Dialogue..11

Promote Critical Thinking 13

Local Engagement..16

Youth Engagement...19

Peace-building Initiatives..22

Counter-Narratives..25

Building Alliances 27

Restructure Socio-political Discourse.........................30

Empower Marginalized Communities 33

Counteract Stereotypes..36

Promote Tolerance and Empathy 39

Build Trust in Law Enforcement 41

Promote Social Integration 44

Encourage Responsible Reporting 47

Create Alternatives 50

Understand the Root Causes 53

Encourage Active Bystanders......................................56

Support Mental Health..59

Early Intervention 62

Develop Resilient Narratives.......................................65

Utilize Technology 67

Focus on Personal Narratives......................................70

Promote Shared Values 73

Address Online Radicalization 76

Advocate for Human Rights 79

Leverage Influencers 82

Develop Individual Resilience..85

Use Positive Messaging 88

Fact-Checking Platforms 91

Support Ex-Extremist Speakers 94

Promote Shared Interests 97

Foster Inter-Generational Dialogue.......................................100

Address Discrimination 103

Counter Hate Speech 106

Emphasize Common Goals..109

Empower Voices of Moderation..112

Create Open Dialogues 115

Endorse Ethical Journalism..118

Fight Against Social Isolation 121

Dismantle Echo Chambers 124

Conclusion...126

About the Author 128

Appendix 130

    Recommend Reading List 130

    Glossary of Terms..131

    Discussion Questions...136

Introduction

In the vast and varied landscape of American politics, it is all too easy to lose sight of the middle ground. The edges of the map, where the extreme elements of both major parties reside, often draw our attention with their loud voices and radical views. Yet, it is crucial to remember that these extremes do not define the entirety of their respective parties. They are but a fraction, albeit a vocal one, of a much larger and more nuanced whole.

This is not a game of "both side-isms". We are not suggesting that the extremes on both sides of the political spectrum are equally dangerous or equally extreme. The scales of extremism are not always balanced, and the dangers they pose can vary significantly. It is a nuanced landscape, one that requires careful navigation and thoughtful consideration.

If there were one "action item to rule them all," perhaps it would be the following: We must resist the temptation to judge a party solely by its most extreme elements. It is an easy trap to fall into, but it is one that we must diligently avoid. And when we see others falling into this trap, we must call them out, regardless of their party affiliation. It is our responsibility to criticize and condemn extreme ideas and figures, especially those within our own in-groups. It is only through this process of self-reflection and critique that we can hope to foster a more balanced and fair political discourse.

This book invites you to learn a new way of thinking, to adopt as many points of view as possible. It encourages you to step outside of your comfort zone, to challenge your preconceived notions, and to engage with perspectives that may differ from your own. It is through this process of exploration and understanding that we can begin to see the full picture of American politics, in all its complexity and diversity.

Within these pages, you will find hundreds of actionable items that you can do or encourage others to do. These are not abstract concepts or theoretical ideas, but practical steps that you can take to make a difference. They are tools for change, for progress, for rebuilding the democracy that we hold dear.

Together, we can navigate the complexities of our political landscape. Together, we can challenge extremism in all its forms. Together, we can save and rebuild democracy. This is our journey, and it starts here.

Promote Media Literacy

In the face of escalating political extremism, promoting media literacy is a vital strategy to combat misinformation and nurture a critical understanding of the information we consume. By empowering individuals to discern reliable news from falsehoods, we can actively contribute to a more informed society. Let's delve into actionable steps that you can take to foster a discerning mindset, distinguish credible sources, and combat the spread of misinformation.

1. Embrace Information Diversity: Embrace a diverse range of news sources, seeking out perspectives from various media outlets. Avoid relying solely on a single source, as this can lead to a skewed understanding of complex issues. By exposing ourselves to diverse viewpoints, we can gain a broader perspective and reduce the risk of falling into echo chambers.

2. Verify Before Sharing: Prioritize fact-checking before sharing news or information on social media. Take the time to investigate the accuracy and credibility of the content. Rely on reputable fact-checking organizations or independent sources to verify claims. By refraining from sharing unverified or sensationalized content, we play a crucial role in preventing the inadvertent spread of misinformation.

3. Develop Critical Thinking Skills: Cultivate critical thinking skills by actively engaging with the news we consume. Ask probing questions about the information presented, including its source, potential biases, supporting evidence, and broader context. Be vigilant for sensationalized or emotionally manipulative content, striving to seek out objective reporting grounded in facts.

4. Understand Media Bias: Familiarize ourselves with the concept of media bias and its impact on news coverage. Recognize that different media outlets may have inherent biases, and that balanced understanding requires exposure to a variety of perspectives. By being aware of media biases, we can better assess the information we encounter and develop a more nuanced understanding of complex issues.

5. Fact-Check Using Reliable Sources: Engage with reputable fact-checking organizations and independent sources to verify the accuracy of information. Ensure that these sources adhere to rigorous standards of journalistic integrity and have a track record of reliability. By basing our understanding on verified facts, we can resist the spread of misinformation and contribute to a more informed public discourse.

6. Share Knowledge and Educate Others: Share our media literacy knowledge with family, friends, and colleagues. Encourage critical thinking, fact-checking, and responsible information sharing. By initiating conversations, organizing workshops, or sharing resources, we can empower others to navigate the media landscape with a discerning eye.

7. Support Independent Journalism: Recognize and support independent journalism outlets that uphold high journalistic standards. Subscribe to or financially contribute to these sources, as they often serve as a valuable counterbalance to mainstream media narratives. By supporting independent journalism, we help maintain a diverse media landscape and foster investigative reporting.

8. Engage in Respectful Online Discussions: Participate in online discussions and debates with civility and respect. Strive to understand differing perspectives and engage in meaningful conversations that promote understanding rather than division. By modeling respectful discourse, we contribute to a healthier online environment.

9. Report Misinformation and Disinformation: Actively report instances of misinformation or disinformation on social media platforms and other relevant channels. By flagging false or misleading content, we aid in the efforts to maintain the integrity of public information spaces.

10. Stay Informed and Stay Vigilant: Stay informed about current events, particularly during critical periods such as elections. Remain vigilant against the manipulation of information and the spread of extremist narratives. By being proactive and discerning consumers of news, we can actively combat political extremism and contribute to a more informed society.

Engage in Dialogue

In our society today, where political extremism seems to be on the rise, engaging in constructive dialogue is a powerful strategy to combat the divisions that plague us. By promoting understanding, empathy, and cooperation among individuals with diverse political ideologies, we can strive to create a more harmonious and inclusive world. Let's explore actionable steps that you can take to foster constructive engagement and bridge the gaps that separate us.

1. Seek Common Ground: Initiate conversations that transcend political boundaries, actively seeking areas of agreement and shared values. By focusing on common ground, we can establish a foundation for understanding and build connections that transcend partisan divides.

2. Cultivate Empathy: Develop the capacity to empathize with others' perspectives by genuinely listening to their experiences and challenges. Strive to understand the underlying motivations and emotions that shape their political beliefs, fostering compassion and promoting meaningful dialogue.

3. Embrace Intellectual Humility: Nurture intellectual humility by recognizing the limitations of our own knowledge and perspectives. Approach discussions with an open mind, acknowledging that we can learn from others, even those with whom we disagree vehemently.

4. Promote Respectful Discourse: Model and encourage respectful discourse by engaging in conversations characterized by civility, patience, and open-mindedness.

Treat individuals with respect, focusing on the merits of their arguments rather than engaging in personal attacks or dismissive rhetoric.

5. Practice Active Listening: Actively listen to others, suspending judgment and giving their ideas a fair hearing. Demonstrate your engagement by asking clarifying questions, reflecting on their viewpoints, and responding thoughtfully.

6. Explore Nuances: Recognize the multifaceted nature of political ideologies and encourage discussions that delve into these complexities. By exploring nuances, we can deepen our understanding of diverse perspectives and challenge simplistic generalizations.

7. Embrace Diversity of Thought: Actively seek out diverse viewpoints and engage with a variety of sources that represent a wide range of political ideologies. Embracing diversity of thought exposes us to new ideas, helps us avoid confirmation bias, and broadens our understanding of complex issues.

8. Use Constructive Language: Choose your words thoughtfully, aiming for clarity and understanding. Communicate ideas in a way that encourages cooperation and fosters a sense of common purpose, steering clear of inflammatory or derogatory language.

9. Reflect on Personal Biases: Engage in introspection and reflect on your own biases and preconceptions. Be willing to challenge and reassess your assumptions, recognizing the influence that cognitive biases can have on your perceptions and interactions.

Promote Critical Thinking

In the fight against political extremism, promoting critical thinking stands as a powerful strategy to equip individuals with the skills to question, analyze, and challenge extremist ideologies. By fostering critical thinking skills in schools and communities, we empower individuals to evaluate information critically, identify logical fallacies, and engage in thoughtful and informed decision-making. Let's explore actionable steps that you can take to contribute to the fight against political extremism through the promotion of critical thinking.

1. Integrate Critical Thinking in Education: Advocate for the integration of critical thinking skills in educational curricula. Support initiatives that emphasize logical reasoning, evidence evaluation, and the ability to engage in respectful and informed debates.

2. Encourage Questioning and Curiosity: Encourage a culture of questioning and curiosity in schools, workplaces, and communities. Foster environments where individuals feel empowered to ask critical questions, challenge assumptions, and seek evidence to support or refute claims.

3. Provide Resources for Media Literacy: Support programs and resources that enhance media literacy skills. Promote the ability to discern reliable news sources, identify bias and misinformation, and engage with media content critically.

4. Organize Workshops and Discussion Forums: Organize workshops, discussion forums, and community events focused on developing critical thinking skills. Provide platforms for individuals to practice critical analysis, engage in respectful debates, and learn from different perspectives.

5. Teach Cognitive Biases Awareness: Educate individuals about cognitive biases and their influence on decision-making. Promote awareness of common biases, such as confirmation bias and groupthink, to encourage a more objective and open-minded approach to evaluating information.

6. Foster Information Literacy: Support initiatives that promote information literacy. Teach individuals how to assess the credibility and reliability of sources, verify information through fact-checking, and distinguish between evidence-based claims and baseless assertions.

7. Encourage Multiple Perspectives: Encourage exposure to multiple perspectives and viewpoints. Foster an environment where individuals actively seek out diverse opinions, engage with different ideologies, and develop empathy and understanding for varying worldviews.

8. Promote Analytical Writing: Promote the development of analytical writing skills that require individuals to critically evaluate and present evidence-based arguments. Encourage writing assignments that foster logical reasoning, evidence evaluation, and coherent argumentation.

9. Engage in Socratic Dialogue: Encourage the practice of Socratic dialogue, where individuals engage in thoughtful questioning and reflective discourse. Create spaces where individuals can explore complex issues, challenge assumptions, and arrive at nuanced understandings through reasoned discussions.

10. Lead by Example: Model critical thinking skills in your own actions and conversations. Demonstrate the ability to question, analyze, and challenge ideas respectfully and constructively. Encourage others to engage in critical thinking through your own thoughtful and well-reasoned approach.

Local Engagement

In the face of growing political extremism, actively engaging in local politics and community organizations can be a powerful strategy to foster trust, understanding, and mutual respect among individuals with diverse viewpoints. By focusing on our immediate communities, we have the opportunity to build connections and bridge divides that contribute to the larger societal discourse. Let's delve into actionable steps that you can take to fight political extremism and promote a more united and harmonious society.

1. Get Involved in Local Politics: Engage in local politics by attending town hall meetings, joining local political groups, or volunteering for political campaigns. By actively participating, we can influence local policy decisions and contribute to shaping a more inclusive and balanced political landscape.

2. Foster Community Organizations: Participate in community organizations that prioritize cooperation, inclusivity, and understanding. These organizations can be based on shared interests, charitable causes, or cultural activities. By working together on common goals, we build relationships and break down barriers among individuals with diverse backgrounds.

3. Listen and Learn: Actively listen to the concerns, perspectives, and experiences of individuals within our local community. Seek opportunities to engage in conversations that foster understanding and empathy. By genuinely hearing others' voices, we can create spaces for dialogue that promote mutual respect and bridge ideological gaps.

4. Collaborate on Local Initiatives: Seek opportunities to collaborate with individuals from different political backgrounds on local initiatives or projects. By focusing on shared goals that benefit the community, we can find common ground and build trust among diverse perspectives.

5. Volunteer for Nonprofit Organizations: Offer your time and skills to local nonprofit organizations that address pressing community needs. Working together towards a common cause helps break down political barriers and strengthens bonds based on shared values and aspirations.

6. Promote Civil Discourse: Model and encourage civil discourse within local political conversations. Engage in discussions with respect, open-mindedness, and a willingness to find common ground. Encourage others to do the same, fostering an environment where diverse opinions can be shared without hostility or animosity.

7. Bridge Divides through Education: Organize or participate in educational events that promote understanding and dialogue among individuals with different political perspectives. Workshops, panel discussions, or community forums can provide opportunities for learning, dispelling misconceptions, and finding areas of agreement.

8. Encourage Voter Education: Promote voter education initiatives within your community. Organize informational sessions on candidates and issues, facilitate voter registration drives, or share unbiased resources that provide accurate information. Empowering individuals with knowledge helps create an informed electorate and strengthens democratic processes.

9. Collaborate on Community Problem-Solving: Engage with diverse individuals in your community to address local challenges collectively. By focusing on problem-solving and finding practical solutions, we can foster a sense of unity and collaboration that transcends political differences.

10. Lead by Example: Embody the values of empathy, respect, and cooperation in your daily interactions within the local community. Lead by example, demonstrating how civil discourse and constructive engagement can bridge political divides and foster a sense of belonging and collective well-being.

Youth Engagement

Amid the growing concern of political extremism, actively engaging the younger generation in political conversations and actions is a powerful strategy to promote inclusivity, representation, and a sense of empowerment. By involving young individuals in political processes, we not only amplify their voices but also nurture a future where diverse perspectives are valued and extremism is countered. Drawing inspiration from thought-provoking writers who have explored the significance of youth engagement, let's delve into actionable steps that you can take to fight political extremism and foster a more inclusive and vibrant political landscape.

1. Foster Open Dialogue: Create spaces for open dialogue with young individuals, encouraging them to express their opinions, concerns, and aspirations regarding political issues. By actively listening to their voices, we demonstrate the importance of their participation and provide a platform for meaningful engagement.

2. Educate on Political Processes: Empower the younger generation by providing them with knowledge about political processes, including voting, civic duties, and the impact of policy decisions. Educate them about the importance of being informed and engaged citizens in shaping the future.

3. Encourage Youth Representation: Advocate for increased youth representation in political institutions, encouraging the inclusion of diverse perspectives in decision-making processes. Support initiatives that promote youth involvement in local councils, community organizations, and advisory boards.

4. Support Youth-Led Organizations: Contribute to and support youth-led organizations that focus on political engagement, activism, and advocacy. Encourage young individuals to create and lead initiatives that address social and political issues they are passionate about, providing them with platforms to enact positive change.

5. Provide Mentorship Opportunities: Offer mentorship and guidance to young individuals interested in political involvement. Share your experiences, insights, and knowledge to help them navigate the complexities of the political landscape and develop their own political identities.

6. Encourage Critical Thinking: Nurture critical thinking skills among the youth, helping them evaluate information critically and discern reliable sources. Encourage them to question assumptions, analyze different perspectives, and form their own well-informed opinions.

7. Facilitate Youth-Led Political Debates: Organize or support youth-led political debates and discussions where young individuals can engage in constructive conversations on current issues. Provide a platform for them to articulate their thoughts, listen to different viewpoints, and foster mutual understanding.

8. Promote Political Education in Schools: Advocate for political education and civics to be included in school curricula. Encourage educational institutions to provide opportunities for students to learn about political systems, public policy, and the importance of political engagement.

9. Organize Youth Forums and Workshops: Arrange forums and workshops where young individuals can learn about political activism, grassroots organizing, and civic participation. Empower them with the necessary skills and knowledge to make a meaningful impact in their communities.

10. Amplify Youth Voices: Actively amplify the voices of young activists and advocates through social media, traditional media, and community platforms. Share their stories, initiatives, and perspectives to ensure their contributions are recognized and valued.

Peace-building Initiatives

Amidst the challenges posed by political extremism, fostering peace-building initiatives rises as a significant course of action to diffuse tensions, promote understanding, and strengthen social cohesion. By actively engaging in efforts to bridge divides between conflicting groups, we can contribute to a more harmonious and inclusive society. Let's delve into actionable steps that you can take to fight political extremism and promote a culture of peace.

1. Cultivate Empathy: Foster empathy by seeking to understand the experiences, perspectives, and grievances of individuals from conflicting groups. Empathy forms the foundation for building connections and breaking down barriers that contribute to extremism.

2. Promote Dialogue: Facilitate constructive dialogue between conflicting groups, providing a platform for open and respectful conversations. Encourage participants to listen actively, share their perspectives, and work towards finding common ground.

3. Encourage Mediation: Encourage the involvement of mediators who are trained in conflict resolution and can help facilitate peaceful discussions between conflicting parties. Mediation provides a neutral space for constructive dialogue and finding mutually beneficial solutions.

4. Foster Intergroup Collaboration: Promote collaborative initiatives that bring together individuals from conflicting groups to work on shared goals or projects. By focusing on common objectives, we can build relationships, foster understanding, and reduce animosity.

5. Support Grassroots Peace-building Organizations: Contribute to and support grassroots organizations that are dedicated to peace-building and reconciliation efforts. These organizations play a vital role in promoting understanding, facilitating dialogue, and implementing initiatives that foster harmony within communities.

6. Engage in Intercultural Exchanges: Actively participate in intercultural exchanges, fostering opportunities for individuals from different backgrounds to interact, learn from one another, and appreciate diverse perspectives. Such exchanges promote understanding, challenge stereotypes, and break down barriers.

7. Advocate for Inclusive Policies: Advocate for inclusive policies that promote equal rights, social justice, and respect for diversity. By supporting policies that value and protect all individuals, we can address root causes of extremism and create an environment conducive to peace.

8. Promote Education for Peace: Support and promote peace education programs that teach conflict resolution, empathy, and the importance of peaceful coexistence. Emphasize the value of dialogue, understanding, and nonviolent communication.

9. Encourage Grassroots Initiatives: Encourage and participate in grassroots initiatives that focus on community engagement, cultural exchange, and activities that promote social cohesion. By empowering individuals at the grassroots level, we can foster a sense of belonging and counter extremist narratives.

10. Lead by Example: Embody the values of peace, understanding, and empathy in your own interactions and relationships. Lead by example, demonstrating how peaceful dialogue and cooperation can bridge divides and promote a culture of inclusivity and respect.

Counter-Narratives

In the fight against political extremism, harnessing the power of counter-narratives becomes a vital strategy to challenge extremist ideologies and uphold democratic norms. By utilizing media and educational platforms, we can actively promote alternative narratives that emphasize inclusivity, tolerance, and the importance of democratic principles. Let's delve into actionable steps that you can take to fight political extremism and contribute to a more resilient and democratic society.

1. Create and Share Compelling Stories: Craft and share stories that showcase the positive aspects of diversity, cooperation, and democratic values. Utilize various media platforms such as social media, blogs, or local publications to amplify these narratives, inspiring others to question extremist ideologies.

2. Engage in Digital Activism: Participate in digital activism by supporting campaigns and initiatives that promote inclusive and democratic values. Utilize social media platforms to share information, resources, and perspectives that challenge extremist narratives and encourage critical thinking.

3. Promote Media Literacy: Educate others about media literacy by sharing resources, organizing workshops, or initiating discussions on how to discern reliable sources and identify extremist propaganda. Foster a critical understanding of media outlets, helping individuals navigate the complex media landscape.

4. Encourage Critical Thinking: Foster critical thinking skills among individuals by encouraging them to question extremist narratives, analyze information critically, and seek multiple perspectives. Promote the importance of evidence-based reasoning and rational discourse.

5. Foster Dialogue and Understanding: Facilitate conversations and dialogues that promote understanding and empathy among individuals with differing viewpoints. Encourage respectful discussions, active listening, and the exchange of ideas to challenge extremist ideologies and foster mutual understanding.

6. Engage in Educational Initiatives: Collaborate with educational institutions and organizations to develop educational initiatives that emphasize democratic values, critical thinking, and the appreciation of diverse perspectives. Support curricula that teach the importance of democratic norms and challenge extremist ideologies.

7. Support Peace-building Efforts: Contribute to peace-building initiatives that aim to address underlying conflicts and grievances. Support organizations working towards reconciliation, conflict resolution, and promoting peaceful coexistence.

8. Lead by Example: Embody democratic values in your own words and actions. Treat others with respect, engage in constructive dialogue, and uphold democratic principles in your personal and professional spheres. By leading by example, you inspire others to follow suit and contribute to the fight against political extremism.

Building Alliances

In the face of political extremism, forging alliances across political, religious, and cultural lines becomes a powerful strategy to create a united front against extremist ideologies. By bringing together civil society organizations, religious institutions, academia, and others, we can collectively work towards fostering understanding, promoting tolerance, and countering divisive narratives. Let's delve into actionable steps that you can take to fight political extremism and foster a more united and inclusive society.

1. Seek Common Ground: Initiate conversations and collaborations that transcend political, religious, and cultural boundaries. Identify shared values and interests, emphasizing the commonalities that bind us together as a society.

2. Foster Interfaith Dialogue: Engage in interfaith dialogue, facilitating conversations among individuals from diverse religious backgrounds. Encourage open-mindedness, respect, and a willingness to learn from one another's traditions and beliefs.

3. Bridge Political Divides: Actively engage with individuals from opposing political ideologies, seeking areas of agreement and common goals. Emphasize the importance of respectful discourse and finding solutions that transcend partisan divides.

4. Support Civil Society Organizations: Contribute to and support civil society organizations that promote inclusivity, social cohesion, and counter extremist narratives.

Volunteer your time, donate resources, or participate in initiatives that foster unity and address societal challenges.

5. Collaborate with Academic Institutions: Collaborate with academic institutions and researchers to promote interdisciplinary studies on extremism, radicalization, and peace-building. Support research initiatives that shed light on the underlying causes of political extremism and identify effective strategies for countering it.

6. Promote Cultural Exchange Programs: Encourage and participate in cultural exchange programs that bring together individuals from diverse backgrounds. These programs foster understanding, appreciation for different cultures, and provide opportunities for building personal connections across borders.

7. Engage with Community Leaders: Reach out to community leaders, including religious leaders, educators, and activists, to initiate conversations on countering extremism. Collaborate on initiatives that promote tolerance, inclusivity, and understanding within the community.

8. Advocate for Intersecting Identities: Advocate for recognition and understanding of individuals with intersecting identities, such as race, religion, gender, or ethnicity. Support initiatives that challenge stereotypes, promote diversity, and celebrate the contributions of individuals from all walks of life.

9. Support Media Efforts: Support media initiatives that strive to present balanced perspectives and counter extremist narratives. Contribute to independent journalism outlets that prioritize responsible reporting and fact-checking, helping to counter misinformation and promote informed public discourse.

10. Organize Joint Events and Workshops: Organize joint events, workshops, and panel discussions that bring together diverse voices to address pressing issues and find common ground. Encourage dialogue, collaboration, and the exchange of ideas among participants.

Restructure Socio-political Discourse

In the fight against political extremism, restructuring socio-political discourse becomes a pivotal strategy to challenge divisive 'us vs. them' mentalities and foster a more inclusive society that values diversity and difference. By advocating for a shift in political language and narrative, we can contribute to a more nuanced understanding of complex issues and promote dialogue that transcends rigid dichotomies. Let's delve into actionable steps that you can take to fight political extremism and restructure the way we engage in socio-political discussions.

1. Promote Inclusive Language: Advocate for the use of inclusive language that acknowledges and respects the diversity of perspectives, identities, and experiences within our society. Encourage individuals to avoid dichotomous rhetoric and instead embrace language that fosters empathy, understanding, and collaboration.

2. Challenge Stereotypes: Actively challenge stereotypes by engaging in conversations that challenge preconceived notions and generalizations. Encourage others to recognize the complexity and individuality of people's experiences, fostering a more nuanced understanding of diverse viewpoints.

3. Encourage Nuanced Debate: Foster an environment that promotes nuanced debate by encouraging individuals to delve into the complexities of issues, rather than resorting to oversimplified arguments. Encourage the exploration of multiple perspectives and the acknowledgment of differing shades of gray.

4. Value Constructive Disagreement: Embrace the concept of constructive disagreement, recognizing that respectful dissent and robust debate are integral to a healthy democracy. Encourage the exploration of different viewpoints and the search for common ground through dialogue.

5. Highlight Shared Goals: Emphasize shared goals and values when engaging in political discussions. Identify common aspirations that unite individuals across different ideologies, focusing on areas of agreement and building bridges rather than perpetuating divisive narratives.

6. Encourage Empathy: Promote empathy by encouraging individuals to listen actively, seek to understand differing perspectives, and consider the experiences and motivations of others. By fostering empathy, we can bridge divides and cultivate a culture of understanding.

7. Challenge Extremist Narratives: Speak out against extremist narratives that perpetuate division and animosity. Counteract them by presenting alternative narratives that emphasize cooperation, understanding, and the importance of finding common ground.

8. Support Intersectionality: Advocate for an intersectional approach that recognizes and values the interconnectedness of various social, economic, and political issues. Promote discussions that highlight the ways in which different aspects of identity intersect and impact experiences within society.

9. Engage in Active Listening: Practice active listening by attentively hearing and considering the perspectives of others. By fostering a culture of active listening, we create space for respectful dialogue and meaningful exchange of ideas.

10. Lead by Example: Exemplify inclusive language, open-mindedness, and respect in your own interactions and conversations. Lead by example, demonstrating how constructive discourse and a willingness to embrace diverse viewpoints can contribute to a more inclusive and empathetic society.

Empower Marginalized Communities

In the battle against political extremism, empowering marginalized communities emerges as a vital strategy to prevent the feelings of resentment and disenfranchisement that often drive individuals towards extremist ideologies. By actively working to empower these communities, we can address systemic inequities, provide opportunities for social and economic advancement, and foster a sense of belonging and inclusion. Let's delve into actionable steps that you can take to fight political extremism and create a more equitable and harmonious society.

1. Advocate for Equal Representation: Advocate for equal representation of marginalized communities in decision-making processes, whether it be in politics, organizations, or other institutions. Support efforts to amplify their voices and ensure their concerns are addressed.

2. Support Access to Education: Advocate for increased access to quality education for marginalized communities. Support initiatives that provide scholarships, mentorship programs, and resources to empower individuals within these communities to pursue educational opportunities.

3. Promote Economic Opportunities: Support initiatives that promote economic opportunities for marginalized communities, such as job training programs, microfinancing, and entrepreneurship support. Encourage businesses and organizations to prioritize diversity and inclusion in their hiring practices.

4. Foster Community Development: Engage in community development projects that uplift marginalized communities, including infrastructure improvements, access to healthcare, and recreational facilities. Collaborate with community leaders and organizations to identify and address specific needs.

5. Amplify Marginalized Voices: Use your platform and privilege to amplify the voices of marginalized individuals and communities. Share their stories, perspectives, and achievements through social media, traditional media, or community events to ensure their narratives are heard and valued.

6. Support Grassroots Organizations: Contribute to and support grassroots organizations that are dedicated to empowering marginalized communities. Donate resources, volunteer time, or offer expertise to initiatives focused on community development, advocacy, and capacity-building.

7. Promote Cultural Exchange and Understanding: Encourage cultural exchange and understanding by actively participating in events and activities that foster dialogue and appreciation for diverse cultures and backgrounds. Engage in conversations that challenge stereotypes and promote inclusivity.

8. Advocate for Policy Changes: Advocate for policy changes that address systemic inequities and promote social justice. Support organizations and initiatives that work towards legislative reforms aimed at improving the lives of marginalized communities.

9. Mentorship and Support: Offer mentorship and support to individuals from marginalized communities, providing guidance, resources, and encouragement to help them overcome challenges and achieve their goals.

10. Promote Allyship and Solidarity: Foster allyship and solidarity by standing up against discrimination, bias, and prejudice. Educate yourself on the experiences and struggles faced by marginalized communities and actively work towards dismantling systems of oppression.

Counteract Stereotypes

In the fight against political extremism, countering stereotypes and dispelling harmful misinformation about different racial, ethnic, or religious groups becomes a crucial strategy to combat divisive ideologies. Stereotypes perpetuate prejudice, discrimination, and exclusion, fueling the very divisions that extremist ideologies thrive upon. Let's delve into actionable steps that you can take to fight political extremism and promote a more inclusive and empathetic society.

1. Educate Yourself: Take the initiative to educate yourself about different racial, ethnic, and religious groups, their diverse histories, cultures, and contributions to society. Seek out reputable sources, engage in thoughtful reading, and challenge your own assumptions and biases.

2. Engage in Interpersonal Connections: Actively seek out opportunities to engage in meaningful interactions with individuals from different racial, ethnic, or religious backgrounds. Build relationships, listen to personal stories, and foster empathy by recognizing the uniqueness and complexity of each individual.

3. Share Personal Experiences: Share your own personal experiences that challenge stereotypes and provide alternative narratives. Use your voice to counteract misinformation and highlight the richness and diversity within different communities.

4. Promote Diversity in Media: Support media outlets and content creators that promote diversity, accurate representation, and counter stereotypes. Share and engage with diverse voices, movies, books, and TV shows that provide authentic portrayals of various racial, ethnic, and religious groups.

5. Challenge Stereotypes in Conversations: When encountering stereotypes in conversations, respectfully challenge them by providing counterexamples and offering alternative perspectives. Encourage critical thinking and open dialogue that challenges preconceived notions.

6. Be Mindful of Language: Pay attention to the language you use and avoid perpetuating stereotypes or engaging in discriminatory language. Foster inclusive and respectful communication that values the unique experiences and identities of individuals.

7. Support Cultural Exchange: Participate in cultural exchange programs, events, and initiatives that foster understanding, appreciation, and collaboration between different racial, ethnic, or religious groups. Actively engage in activities that celebrate diversity and promote cross-cultural understanding.

8. Advocate for Inclusive Education: Advocate for inclusive education that accurately represents diverse cultures, histories, and perspectives. Support curriculum reforms that promote cultural competency and challenge stereotypes within educational institutions.

9. Foster Intergroup Dialogue: Organize or participate in intergroup dialogue sessions that bring together individuals from different racial, ethnic, or religious backgrounds. Encourage open and respectful conversations that aim to bridge divides and promote understanding.

10. Lead by Example: Embody the values of inclusivity, empathy, and understanding in your own actions and interactions. Challenge stereotypes, celebrate diversity, and treat others with respect and dignity. By leading by example, you inspire others to question stereotypes and embrace a more inclusive mindset.

Promote Tolerance and Empathy

In the battle against political extremism, promoting tolerance and empathy serves as a crucial strategy to cultivate understanding, bridge divides, and counter the divisive narratives that fuel extremist ideologies. Let's delve into actionable steps that you can take to fight political extremism and foster a more compassionate and inclusive society.

1. Support Educational Programs: Advocate for the inclusion of educational programs that promote tolerance, empathy, and understanding in school curricula. Support initiatives that teach conflict resolution, cultural competency, and appreciation for diverse perspectives.

2. Engage in Interfaith and Intercultural Dialogues: Participate in interfaith and intercultural dialogues that encourage the exchange of ideas, foster empathy, and build bridges between different religious and cultural communities. Actively listen and seek to understand others' experiences and beliefs.

3. Promote Public Campaigns: Support and participate in public campaigns that promote tolerance, empathy, and respect for diversity. Use social media platforms, community events, and traditional media outlets to share positive messages that challenge divisive narratives.

4. Encourage Cultural Exchanges: Encourage and participate in cultural exchange programs that foster mutual understanding and appreciation for different cultures and traditions. Embrace opportunities to learn from and engage with individuals from diverse backgrounds.

5. Practice Active Listening: Practice active listening by attentively hearing others' perspectives without judgment or interruption. Seek to understand their experiences and emotions, fostering empathy and promoting constructive dialogue.

6. Promote Empathetic Language: Use language that reflects empathy and respect when discussing sensitive or controversial topics. Avoid derogatory language or personal attacks, and instead focus on fostering understanding and building connections.

7. Volunteer in Community Organizations: Volunteer your time and skills in community organizations that promote tolerance, inclusion, and social cohesion. Contribute to initiatives that bridge gaps, support marginalized communities, and foster a sense of belonging for all.

8. Engage in Community Service: Engage in community service activities that bring together individuals from diverse backgrounds. Collaborate on projects that address community needs and foster connections among community members.

9. Lead by Example: Embody tolerance and empathy in your own actions and interactions. Treat others with kindness, respect, and dignity, regardless of their backgrounds or beliefs. Model inclusive behaviors and inspire others to follow suit.

Build Trust in Law Enforcement

In the pursuit of combating political extremism, building trust between communities and law enforcement emerges as a crucial strategy. When there is a strong foundation of trust, communities are more likely to cooperate with law enforcement agencies, leading to increased safety and a reduction in extremist activities. Let's delve into actionable steps that you can take to foster better relationships between communities and law enforcement, contributing to the fight against political extremism.

1. Promote Community-Police Partnerships: Advocate for and participate in community-police partnerships that facilitate open communication and collaboration. Support initiatives that bring law enforcement officers and community members together to address shared concerns and build mutual understanding.

2. Encourage Cultural Competency Training: Advocate for cultural competency training within law enforcement agencies to foster an understanding of diverse communities and their unique needs. Support programs that promote empathy, respect, and effective communication.

3. Foster Dialogue and Listening Sessions: Organize and participate in dialogue and listening sessions between law enforcement and community members. Create safe spaces where individuals can express their concerns, share their experiences, and engage in constructive conversations with law enforcement representatives.

4. Support Community Policing Initiatives: Support community policing initiatives that prioritize building relationships, proactive problem-solving, and crime prevention. Collaborate with law enforcement agencies to identify community-specific needs and implement tailored strategies.

5. Volunteer for Police-Community Collaborative Programs: Volunteer for programs that foster collaboration between law enforcement and community members, such as community watch programs or youth mentoring initiatives. Contribute to efforts that promote positive interactions and build trust.

6. Advocate for Accountability and Transparency: Advocate for accountability and transparency within law enforcement agencies. Support measures that promote fair and just practices, unbiased investigations, and meaningful consequences for misconduct.

7. Promote Restorative Justice Approaches: Advocate for the implementation of restorative justice approaches within the criminal justice system. Support programs that prioritize healing, rehabilitation, and community reconciliation, fostering trust and reducing recidivism.

8. Engage in Neighborhood Initiatives: Engage in neighborhood initiatives that promote community cohesion and safety. Participate in events such as block parties, neighborhood clean-ups, or crime prevention workshops, fostering connections between residents and law enforcement.

9. Encourage Diversity in Law Enforcement: Advocate for diversity and inclusion within law enforcement agencies. Support initiatives that recruit individuals from diverse backgrounds, ensuring that law enforcement reflects the communities they serve, thereby enhancing trust and understanding.

10. Build Bridges through Positive Interactions: Take the initiative to build bridges through positive interactions with law enforcement officers. Express appreciation for their service, engage in respectful conversations, and seek opportunities to collaborate on community projects.

Promote Social Integration

In the battle against political extremism, promoting social integration assumes an essential tactic to counter social fragmentation and foster a cohesive and inclusive society. By supporting initiatives that bring diverse communities together, we can bridge divides, cultivate understanding, and reduce the conditions that fuel extremist ideologies. Let's delve into actionable steps that you can take to promote social integration and contribute to the fight against political extremism.

1. Embrace Diversity: Embrace and celebrate diversity within your own community and beyond. Recognize the value of different cultures, traditions, and perspectives, fostering an inclusive mindset that appreciates the richness diversity brings.

2. Participate in Community Events: Actively participate in community events that bring together individuals from diverse backgrounds. Attend cultural festivals, neighborhood gatherings, or public forums to foster connections and promote understanding among different communities.

3. Support Language Learning: Support language learning initiatives that help individuals from different backgrounds communicate and connect more effectively. Volunteer as a language tutor or promote resources that facilitate language acquisition, encouraging intercultural dialogue.

4. Engage in Intercultural Exchanges: Seek opportunities to engage in intercultural exchanges, such as exchange programs, interfaith dialogues, or community workshops. Actively listen and learn from others, cultivating empathy and understanding.

5. Encourage Collaboration and Cooperation: Encourage collaboration and cooperation among diverse groups by supporting projects that bring individuals from different backgrounds together. Foster partnerships that address shared challenges and promote collective well-being.

6. Create Inclusive Spaces: Advocate for the creation of inclusive spaces in your community, where individuals from all backgrounds feel welcome and valued. Support initiatives that provide accessible resources, facilities, and services to foster social integration.

7. Promote Cross-Cultural Understanding: Promote cross-cultural understanding by organizing educational events or workshops that facilitate intercultural dialogue. Encourage learning about different cultures, traditions, and customs, fostering empathy and appreciation for diversity.

8. Support Refugee and Migrant Integration: Support organizations and initiatives that assist in the integration of refugees and migrants into local communities. Provide assistance, resources, or mentorship to help newcomers navigate their new environment and feel supported.

9. Foster Intergenerational Connections: Foster intergenerational connections by encouraging dialogue and collaboration between different age groups. Promote initiatives that facilitate mentorship, knowledge-sharing, and intergenerational activities, strengthening community bonds.

10. Practice Inclusive Socializing: Actively practice inclusive socializing by engaging with individuals from diverse backgrounds in social settings. Attend events, gatherings, or volunteer activities that encourage interactions with people of different cultures, fostering understanding and connection.

Encourage Responsible Reporting

In the fight against political extremism, encouraging responsible reporting on extremist activities by working with media outlets acquires importance as a central approach to counter sensationalism and inadvertent promotion of extremist groups. Responsible reporting plays a pivotal role in shaping public perceptions and understanding of extremist ideologies, highlighting the need for accurate, balanced, and thoughtful coverage. Let's delve into actionable steps that you can take to promote responsible reporting and contribute to the fight against political extremism.

1. Promote Media Literacy: Advocate for media literacy programs that equip individuals with the skills to critically evaluate news sources, discern reliable information from misinformation, and recognize the potential biases present in media coverage.

2. Support Independent Journalism: Support independent journalism outlets that prioritize responsible reporting and fact-checking. Subscribe to reputable news sources and contribute to their sustainability to ensure that reliable information reaches a wider audience.

3. Engage in Constructive Feedback: Engage with media outlets through letters, emails, or social media to provide constructive feedback on their coverage of extremist activities. Encourage them to maintain journalistic integrity, avoid sensationalism, and provide balanced perspectives.

4. Encourage Contextual Reporting: Advocate for contextual reporting that goes beyond sensational headlines and provides in-depth analysis of the root causes, ideologies, and historical context behind extremist activities. Promote reporting that examines underlying societal issues and offers comprehensive understanding.

5. Support Investigative Journalism: Support investigative journalism that uncovers the motivations, networks, and methods of extremist groups. Contribute to organizations that fund investigative reporting and expose the complexities of extremism to the public.

6. Raise Awareness about Media Bias: Educate others about media bias and its potential impact on shaping public opinion. Encourage discussions on the importance of seeking multiple perspectives, fact-checking, and cross-referencing sources to form a more comprehensive understanding.

7. Promote Ethical Reporting Standards: Advocate for ethical reporting standards within media organizations. Support initiatives that promote journalistic integrity, accuracy, objectivity, and sensitivity when reporting on sensitive and potentially divisive issues.

8. Share Reliable Information: Share reliable information from credible sources on social media platforms or in personal conversations. Encourage others to critically evaluate the information they consume and verify facts before sharing them.

9. Encourage Media Accountability: Hold media outlets accountable for responsible reporting by supporting initiatives that monitor and evaluate their coverage of extremist activities. Promote transparency, accuracy, and accountability in media practices.

10. Foster Media-Community Partnerships: Foster partnerships between media outlets and local communities to ensure accurate and comprehensive reporting of extremist activities. Encourage collaboration that incorporates community perspectives, reducing the risk of misrepresentation or sensationalism.

Create Alternatives

In the fight against political extremism, creating alternatives to radical ideologies becomes a crucial strategy to address the underlying social, political, and economic issues that extremist groups claim to solve. By offering viable alternatives and addressing the root causes of discontent, we can provide individuals with pathways towards constructive engagement and prevent them from being drawn into extremist ideologies. Let's delve into actionable steps that you can take to create alternatives and contribute to the fight against political extremism.

1. Advocate for Social Justice: Advocate for social justice by supporting initiatives that address inequality, discrimination, and marginalization. Join or support organizations that work towards creating inclusive societies and dismantling systemic barriers that fuel extremist narratives.

2. Promote Civic Engagement: Encourage civic engagement by participating in community organizations, volunteering for political campaigns, and supporting initiatives that promote active citizenship. Provide avenues for individuals to contribute to positive change within their communities.

3. Support Economic Opportunities: Support economic opportunities for marginalized individuals and communities by advocating for policies that foster job creation, entrepreneurship, and equitable access to resources. Engage in initiatives that promote economic empowerment and reduce socio-economic disparities.

4. Foster Education and Critical Thinking: Foster education and critical thinking by supporting programs that provide quality education, emphasize analytical skills, and promote diverse perspectives. Encourage lifelong learning and the development of critical thinking abilities to equip individuals with the tools to challenge extremist ideologies.

5. Provide Mentorship and Guidance: Offer mentorship and guidance to individuals who may be vulnerable to extremist ideologies. Support mentorship programs that provide positive role models, offer guidance on personal and professional development, and encourage critical thinking and empathy.

6. Encourage Dialogue and Debate: Encourage dialogue and debate on societal issues, allowing for a range of perspectives to be heard and critically examined. Foster spaces where respectful and constructive discussions can take place, challenging extremist narratives and providing opportunities for alternative viewpoints to emerge.

7. Strengthen Social Support Systems: Advocate for and support the strengthening of social support systems that address mental health, social isolation, and feelings of disenfranchisement. Collaborate with community organizations and mental health professionals to ensure individuals have access to the support they need.

8. Promote Cultural Understanding: Promote cultural understanding and appreciation by engaging in cultural exchange programs, participating in intercultural events, and supporting initiatives that celebrate diversity. Foster an environment that values cultural differences and promotes cross-cultural understanding and cooperation.

9. Engage in Collaborative Problem-Solving: Engage in collaborative problem-solving efforts that address the root causes of social, political, and economic issues. Seek opportunities to work with diverse stakeholders, including policymakers, community leaders, and advocacy groups, to develop sustainable solutions.

10. Lead by Example: Lead by example by embodying the values of inclusivity, empathy, and constructive engagement in your own actions and interactions. Model the behavior you wish to see, fostering a culture of tolerance, respect, and cooperation.

Understand the Root Causes

In the fight against political extremism, understanding the root causes of extremism serves as a crucial strategy to develop effective countermeasures. By carrying out research and data analysis, we can gain deeper insights into the underlying factors that contribute to the rise of extremism and adapt our strategies accordingly. Let's delve into actionable steps that you can take to contribute to the fight against political extremism by understanding its root causes.

1. Stay Informed: Stay informed about current events, political developments, and social trends through reliable news sources, academic research, and data-driven analyses. Cultivate a well-rounded understanding of the complex factors that contribute to extremism.

2. Support Research Initiatives: Support research initiatives focused on understanding the root causes of extremism. Contribute to organizations that conduct interdisciplinary studies, promote evidence-based approaches, and provide insights into the socio-political, economic, and psychological factors underlying extremist ideologies.

3. Engage in Data Analysis: Develop skills in data analysis to examine patterns, trends, and correlations related to extremism. Utilize available datasets and tools to identify socio-economic disparities, demographic factors, or historical contexts that may contribute to the rise of extremist ideologies.

4. Foster Cross-disciplinary Collaboration: Foster collaboration between different fields of study, including psychology, sociology, political science, economics, and anthropology. Encourage interdisciplinary dialogues and joint research projects to gain comprehensive insights into the root causes of extremism.

5. Support Community-based Research: Support community-based research initiatives that aim to understand local dynamics, grievances, and challenges that contribute to the vulnerability of certain communities to extremist ideologies. Collaborate with researchers, community leaders, and organizations to gather insights directly from affected communities.

6. Promote Evidence-based Policies: Advocate for evidence-based policies that address the root causes of extremism. Support policymakers who rely on research and data to inform decision-making and allocate resources towards effective prevention and intervention strategies.

7. Encourage Inclusive Dialogue: Encourage inclusive dialogue that brings together experts, community leaders, and individuals with diverse perspectives to discuss the root causes of extremism. Foster an environment that welcomes open and respectful discussions, challenging assumptions, and exploring potential solutions.

8. Share Research Findings: Share research findings and insights on the root causes of extremism with a wider audience. Utilize social media, community events, and public forums to disseminate knowledge, raise awareness, and foster informed discussions.

9. Promote Long-term Monitoring: Advocate for long-term monitoring and evaluation of the effectiveness of strategies addressing the root causes of extremism. Support initiatives that measure the impact of interventions and inform policy adjustments based on evidence and lessons learned.

10. Encourage Continued Learning: Foster a culture of continued learning and intellectual curiosity. Stay updated on the latest research, attend conferences, workshops, and lectures that explore the root causes of extremism. Engage in conversations with experts and fellow community members to deepen understanding and refine strategies.

Encourage Active Bystanders

In the fight against political extremism, encouraging individuals to become active bystanders plays a critical role in early detection and prevention. By training people to recognize signs of radicalization and equipping them with the necessary tools to respond effectively and safely, we empower them to intervene and potentially redirect individuals away from extremist ideologies. Let's explore actionable steps that you can take to contribute to the fight against political extremism by encouraging active bystanders.

1. Raise Awareness: Raise awareness about the importance of active bystanders in preventing and countering extremism. Utilize various platforms, such as community gatherings, social media, and educational institutions, to promote discussions and share information about the role of bystanders in early intervention.

2. Educate and Train: Promote educational programs and training initiatives that equip individuals with the knowledge and skills to recognize signs of radicalization. Support workshops, seminars, and online resources that provide guidance on effective strategies for intervention and engagement.

3. Foster Trust and Relationships: Encourage the development of trusting relationships within communities. Foster connections among neighbors, colleagues, and community members to create environments where individuals feel comfortable discussing their concerns and seeking support.

4. Cultivate Active Listening Skills: Promote active listening skills that enable individuals to engage in empathetic and non-judgmental conversations. Encourage open dialogue, where people can express their views and concerns without fear of stigma or reprisal.

5. Provide Safe Reporting Channels: Advocate for the establishment of safe reporting channels where individuals can share their concerns about radicalization anonymously. Support community organizations and helplines that offer confidential platforms for reporting and seeking guidance.

6. Collaborate with Local Authorities: Encourage collaboration between community members and local authorities, such as law enforcement agencies and social service providers. Foster partnerships that facilitate information sharing, training opportunities, and coordinated responses to potential cases of radicalization.

7. Promote Social Support Networks: Support the development of social support networks that provide assistance to individuals at risk of radicalization or those affected by extremist ideologies. Collaborate with community organizations to establish mentoring programs, peer support groups, or counseling services.

8. Disseminate Educational Resources: Disseminate educational resources that outline the warning signs and behavioral indicators of radicalization. Share information through community centers, schools, workplaces, and online platforms to increase awareness and enable early identification.

9. Encourage Community Engagement: Encourage community members to actively engage with individuals who may be susceptible to extremist ideologies. Foster connections through mentorship, cultural activities, sports clubs, or youth programs that provide positive outlets and alternative perspectives.

10. Support Rehabilitation and Reintegration: Support programs and initiatives that focus on the rehabilitation and reintegration of individuals who have been influenced by extremist ideologies. Advocate for access to counseling, education, job training, and community support to facilitate their transition back into society.

Support Mental Health

In the fight against political extremism, addressing mental health issues stands as a crucial strategy to prevent individuals from falling prey to extremist recruitment tactics. Mental health challenges can leave individuals more susceptible to manipulation, feelings of isolation, and a search for belonging that extremist groups may exploit. Let's delve into actionable steps that you can take to contribute to the fight against political extremism by supporting mental health.

1. Promote Mental Health Awareness: Raise awareness about mental health issues and the impact they can have on individuals' susceptibility to extremist recruitment. Initiate conversations, organize educational events, and share resources that destigmatize mental health and promote understanding.

2. Support Accessible Mental Health Services: Advocate for improved access to affordable and accessible mental health services. Support initiatives that prioritize mental health funding, community-based clinics, and helplines that provide confidential and non-judgmental support.

3. Encourage Seeking Help: Encourage individuals to seek help for mental health concerns by promoting the importance of early intervention and destigmatizing help-seeking behaviors. Share personal stories and experiences to inspire others to seek professional support when needed.

4. Foster Supportive Communities: Create and foster supportive communities that prioritize mental well-being.

Establish spaces where individuals can openly discuss their mental health challenges, find support, and connect with others who may be facing similar struggles.

5. Advocate for Mental Health Education: Advocate for the inclusion of mental health education in schools, workplaces, and community programs. Support initiatives that equip individuals with the knowledge and skills to identify mental health challenges, provide appropriate support, and promote self-care.

6. Combat Social Isolation: Combat social isolation by promoting inclusive environments that foster social connections and a sense of belonging. Encourage community engagement, organize social activities, and create opportunities for meaningful interactions to reduce feelings of isolation.

7. Support Peer-to-Peer Networks: Support peer-to-peer networks that provide spaces for individuals to support each other in their mental health journeys. Encourage the establishment of support groups, online communities, and mentoring programs that promote shared experiences and mutual support.

8. Promote Resilience and Coping Skills: Promote resilience and coping skills to enhance mental well-being. Support initiatives that teach individuals healthy coping mechanisms, stress management techniques, and emotional regulation strategies.

9. Advocate for Holistic Approaches: Advocate for holistic approaches to mental health that consider the social, cultural, and environmental factors influencing well-being. Support initiatives that address systemic inequalities, promote social justice, and create supportive structures for marginalized communities.

10. Engage in Self-Care: Encourage individuals to prioritize self-care and mental well-being in their daily lives. Promote practices such as mindfulness, physical activity, healthy sleep habits, and engaging in activities that bring joy and fulfillment.

Early Intervention

In the fight against political extremism, establishing early intervention programs establishes itself as a critical maneuver to identify and assist individuals showing signs of radicalization. By creating accessible channels such as hotlines or community programs, friends or family members can reach out for help and support. Inspired by insightful thinkers who have highlighted the importance of early intervention, let's explore actionable steps that you can take to contribute to the fight against political extremism through early intervention.

1. Raise Awareness: Raise awareness about the signs and indicators of radicalization within communities. Initiate discussions, share educational materials, and organize informational sessions to empower individuals to recognize and respond to early warning signs.

2. Establish Supportive Hotlines: Advocate for the establishment of hotlines or helplines dedicated to supporting individuals who suspect or observe signs of radicalization in their friends or family members. Promote these resources to ensure they are widely known and accessible.

3. Provide Training and Resources: Support initiatives that provide training and resources to equip individuals with the knowledge and skills to identify signs of radicalization and respond appropriately. Collaborate with community organizations and experts to develop educational programs.

4. Strengthen Community Connections: Strengthen community connections by fostering open lines of communication among neighbors, colleagues, and community members. Encourage supportive networks where individuals feel comfortable reaching out for help and guidance.

5. Foster Trust and Confidentiality: Emphasize the importance of trust and confidentiality in early intervention efforts. Create safe spaces where individuals can share their concerns without fear of judgment or retaliation, ensuring privacy and sensitivity throughout the process.

6. Establish Community Programs: Advocate for the establishment of community programs that facilitate early intervention and provide support to individuals showing signs of radicalization. Collaborate with local authorities, community leaders, and mental health professionals to develop and implement these programs effectively.

7. Promote Family Engagement: Promote family engagement in early intervention efforts by encouraging open and non-judgmental communication. Provide resources and support networks for families to seek guidance and assistance when they suspect their loved ones may be at risk of radicalization.

8. Educate on Risk Factors: Educate individuals about the risk factors associated with radicalization, including social isolation, identity crises, and exposure to extremist content. Promote understanding of the underlying vulnerabilities that can contribute to susceptibility to radical ideologies.

9. Support Rehabilitation Programs: Support rehabilitation programs that focus on intervention and reintegration of individuals who have been radicalized. Advocate for access to counseling, mentorship, vocational training, and community support to aid their disengagement from extremist ideologies.

10. Collaborate with Local Authorities: Collaborate with local authorities and law enforcement agencies to ensure effective coordination and communication in early intervention efforts. Encourage the development of protocols and guidelines for identifying, reporting, and responding to cases of radicalization.

Develop Resilient Narratives

In the fight against political extremism, developing resilient narratives stands as a crucial strategy to counteract extremist ideologies. By crafting and propagating narratives that celebrate unity, diversity, tolerance, and democratic values, we can provide individuals with alternative stories that challenge extremist narratives and promote a more inclusive and harmonious society. Let's delve into actionable steps that you can take to contribute to the fight against political extremism through the development of resilient narratives.

1. Understand the Power of Narratives: Recognize the profound impact narratives have on shaping beliefs, values, and actions. Engage in research, read diverse literature, and explore different cultural perspectives to develop a deeper understanding of the power and influence of narratives.

2. Promote Positive Stories: Actively promote and share positive stories that celebrate unity, diversity, tolerance, and democratic values. Highlight narratives that showcase individuals and communities working together, overcoming challenges, and promoting social cohesion.

3. Amplify Diverse Voices: Amplify diverse voices by sharing and uplifting stories from individuals of various backgrounds and perspectives. Encourage platforms that provide space for marginalized voices to be heard and ensure a more inclusive representation of experiences and narratives.

4. Foster Intercommunity Dialogue: Facilitate dialogue and understanding between different communities and cultures. Support initiatives that bring people together to share their stories, engage in open conversations, and foster empathy, respect, and mutual understanding.

5. Collaborate with Artists and Writers: Collaborate with artists, writers, and creative professionals to develop narratives that counter extremist ideologies. Support their work and initiatives that promote inclusive storytelling, challenging stereotypes, and fostering empathy.

6. Utilize Digital Platforms: Utilize digital platforms and social media to disseminate resilient narratives. Share positive stories, engage in constructive discussions, and counteract extremist content by offering alternative viewpoints and narratives.

7. Engage in Storytelling Education: Promote storytelling education that emphasizes critical thinking, empathy, and media literacy. Support programs and workshops that equip individuals with the skills to analyze narratives, distinguish reliable information from misinformation, and critically engage with media.

8. Foster Cross-Cultural Exchanges: Foster cross-cultural exchanges that promote understanding and appreciation for different perspectives. Encourage travel, cultural immersion experiences, and intercultural programs that facilitate encounters and dialogue between diverse communities.

9. Encourage Personal Narratives: Encourage individuals to share their personal narratives and experiences, fostering a sense of connection and empathy. Promote platforms that provide opportunities for individuals to express their stories and contribute to the broader narrative landscape.

Utilize Technology

In the fight against political extremism, harnessing the power of technology and engaging in post-conflict rebuilding efforts stand as crucial strategies to prevent the rise and spread of extremist ideologies. By utilizing AI and machine learning to monitor online activities for signs of radicalization, while respecting privacy rights, we can identify and intervene in potential cases early on. Additionally, engaging in post-conflict rebuilding and reconciliation efforts helps to address the underlying grievances and social divisions that can fuel the growth of extremism. Let's explore actionable steps that you can take to contribute to the fight against political extremism through the utilization of technology and engagement in post-conflict rebuilding.

1. Support Ethical AI Development: Advocate for the development and implementation of ethical AI systems that monitor and analyze online activities for signs of radicalization. Support initiatives that prioritize privacy rights, transparency, and accountability to ensure responsible use of technology.

2. Promote Digital Literacy: Promote digital literacy programs that equip individuals with the skills to navigate online spaces critically. Support initiatives that educate people on identifying extremist content, reporting harmful activities, and engaging in responsible online behavior.

3. Report Extremist Content: Encourage individuals to report extremist content and activities they encounter online through proper channels. Raise awareness about reporting mechanisms provided by platforms and law enforcement agencies to facilitate swift intervention and removal of harmful content.

4. Support Research and Development: Support research and development efforts focused on leveraging AI and machine learning to identify patterns of radicalization online. Encourage collaboration between technology experts, researchers, and policymakers to refine and improve detection algorithms.

5. Advocate for Post-Conflict Rebuilding: Advocate for post-conflict rebuilding efforts in areas affected by conflict. Support initiatives that prioritize social cohesion, community development, and reconciliation to address the root causes of conflict and prevent the emergence of extremist ideologies.

6. Promote Intercommunity Dialogue: Promote dialogue and understanding between communities that have experienced conflict. Encourage initiatives that facilitate open discussions, cultural exchanges, and shared experiences to bridge divides and promote empathy and reconciliation.

7. Support Rehabilitation and Reintegration: Support programs that focus on the rehabilitation and reintegration of individuals affected by conflict and radicalization. Advocate for access to counseling, vocational training, education, and community support to aid in their successful transition and disengagement from extremist ideologies.

8. Volunteer in Post-Conflict Areas: Consider volunteering or supporting organizations working on post-conflict rebuilding projects. Engage in activities that promote social healing, infrastructure development, and the empowerment of affected communities to prevent the resurgence of extremist ideologies.

9. Advocate for Policy Change: Advocate for policy changes that prioritize the prevention of radicalization, support technological advancements, and allocate resources to post-conflict rebuilding efforts. Collaborate with local and national policymakers to ensure the implementation of effective strategies.

10. Foster Cross-Cultural Understanding: Foster cross-cultural understanding and empathy by engaging with diverse communities, cultures, and perspectives. Embrace opportunities for cultural exchange, dialogue, and collaboration to challenge stereotypes and promote inclusivity.

Focus on Personal Narratives

In the fight against political extremism, focusing on personal narratives becomes a powerful strategy to foster understanding, empathy, and challenge dehumanizing stereotypes. By encouraging the sharing of personal narratives between different communities, we create opportunities for individuals to connect on a human level, recognize shared experiences, and challenge the divisive narratives that fuel extremism. Let's explore actionable steps that you can take to contribute to the fight against political extremism through the focus on personal narratives.

1. Create Safe Spaces for Storytelling: Establish safe spaces where individuals from diverse communities can share their personal narratives without fear of judgment or discrimination. Encourage open and respectful dialogue, providing platforms for individuals to express their experiences, perspectives, and challenges.

2. Promote Empathy and Active Listening: Promote empathy and active listening skills to foster a deeper understanding of others' lived experiences. Encourage individuals to listen attentively and reflect on different narratives, embracing diverse viewpoints and challenging preconceived notions.

3. Organize Narrative-Sharing Events: Organize events that facilitate the sharing of personal narratives, such as storytelling workshops, cultural exchanges, or community gatherings. Provide opportunities for individuals to engage in meaningful conversations and connect through their stories.

4. Embrace Digital Storytelling Platforms: Embrace digital storytelling platforms, such as blogs, podcasts, or social media channels, to amplify personal narratives and reach wider audiences. Encourage individuals to share their stories online, creating a virtual space for connection, understanding, and dialogue.

5. Foster Cross-Cultural Storytelling: Facilitate cross-cultural storytelling initiatives that promote understanding and empathy between different communities. Encourage individuals from diverse backgrounds to share their narratives, fostering a sense of shared humanity and challenging stereotypes.

6. Support Media Projects that Humanize Others: Support media projects that aim to humanize individuals from marginalized communities or groups often targeted by extremist narratives. Back initiatives that provide a platform for authentic storytelling, challenging dehumanization and promoting empathy.

7. Encourage Personal Reflection and Expression: Encourage individuals to engage in personal reflection and self-expression through writing, art, or other creative outlets. Foster a culture that values introspection and encourages individuals to explore and share their own narratives.

8. Collaborate with Educational Institutions: Collaborate with educational institutions to integrate personal narratives into curricula and educational materials. Support initiatives that expose students to diverse stories and experiences, promoting empathy, respect, and critical thinking.

9. Engage in Intergenerational Dialogue: Facilitate intergenerational dialogue where individuals from different age groups share their personal narratives. Encourage the exchange of wisdom, experiences, and perspectives, fostering understanding and bridging generational gaps.

Promote Shared Values

In the fight against political extremism, promoting shared values becomes a powerful strategy to bridge political and cultural divides, foster a sense of shared identity, and cultivate cooperation. By highlighting and promoting values that transcend these divisions, we can create a common ground where individuals from diverse backgrounds can come together, find commonalities, and work towards a more inclusive and harmonious society. Let's explore actionable steps that you can take to contribute to the fight against political extremism through the promotion of shared values.

1. Identify Universal Values: Identify and emphasize universal values that are shared across cultures, ideologies, and political spectrums. Promote values such as human dignity, compassion, justice, freedom, and respect for diversity as foundational principles that can bridge divides and foster cooperation.

2. Lead by Example: Embody and exemplify the shared values you wish to promote. Demonstrate these values in your actions, interactions, and decisions, inspiring others to follow suit and creating a ripple effect within your community.

3. Encourage Dialogue and Exchange: Encourage dialogue and exchange of perspectives that revolve around shared values. Facilitate conversations that allow individuals to find common ground, discover shared aspirations, and build understanding through respectful engagement.

4. Collaborate on Community Projects: Collaborate with individuals from different backgrounds on community projects that reflect shared values. Engage in initiatives that promote social cohesion, environmental sustainability, or support for vulnerable populations, fostering a sense of collective purpose and cooperation.

5. Promote Interfaith and Intercultural Understanding: Promote interfaith and intercultural understanding by actively seeking opportunities to learn about different belief systems and cultural practices. Attend cultural events, visit places of worship, and engage in respectful discussions that help break down stereotypes and build bridges of understanding.

6. Support Civic Education: Support civic education initiatives that emphasize shared values and democratic principles. Advocate for inclusive educational curricula that highlight the importance of dialogue, collaboration, and respect for diverse perspectives.

7. Engage in Grassroots Activism: Engage in grassroots activism that promotes shared values and addresses social challenges. Join or support organizations working towards causes aligned with shared values, amplifying collective efforts for positive change.

8. Amplify Shared Values in Media: Encourage media outlets to highlight stories and narratives that exemplify shared values. Support media platforms that promote cooperation, empathy, and understanding, fostering a more balanced and inclusive representation of societal perspectives.

9. Volunteer in Community Service: Volunteer in community service projects that embody shared values.

Engage in initiatives that address local needs, promote inclusivity, and create opportunities for individuals from different backgrounds to collaborate towards a common goal.

Address Online Radicalization

In the battle against political extremism, addressing online radicalization stands as a critical strategy to combat the spread of extremist ideologies and prevent their harmful effects. Online platforms have become fertile grounds for recruitment, propaganda dissemination, and radicalization processes. Therefore, it is imperative that we take action to counter online radicalization, whether through monitoring, intervention, or regulation of online spaces. Let's explore actionable steps that you can take to contribute to the fight against political extremism through addressing online radicalization.

1. Support Digital Literacy Education: Advocate for digital literacy education programs that equip individuals with the skills necessary to navigate the online world critically and responsibly. Promote initiatives that teach individuals how to identify and evaluate extremist content, discern reliable sources of information, and understand the potential consequences of their online actions.

2. Foster Online Community Engagement: Encourage online community engagement that fosters constructive dialogue and provides alternative narratives to extremist ideologies. Support platforms and initiatives that facilitate meaningful discussions, encourage diverse perspectives, and promote empathy and understanding.

3. Promote Responsible Online Reporting: Encourage responsible online reporting by individuals who encounter extremist content or witness signs of radicalization. Raise awareness about reporting mechanisms provided by online platforms and law enforcement agencies, enabling timely intervention and removal of harmful content.

4. Support Online Intervention Programs: Support the development and implementation of online intervention programs that provide support, counseling, and resources for individuals at risk of radicalization. Advocate for increased funding and accessibility to such programs, ensuring that those in need can access help in a timely manner.

5. Collaborate with Tech Companies: Advocate for collaboration between individuals, civil society organizations, and technology companies to address online radicalization. Encourage tech companies to invest in robust content moderation systems, implement algorithms that detect extremist content, and establish transparent policies regarding the removal of harmful materials.

6. Engage in Online Counter-Narratives: Engage in the creation and dissemination of online counter-narratives that challenge extremist ideologies. Use social media platforms, blogs, and other online channels to share stories, information, and perspectives that promote tolerance, understanding, and the values of democracy and respect for human rights.

7. Support Legislation and Regulation: Advocate for legislation and regulation that address online radicalization without compromising freedom of speech. Support measures that hold online platforms accountable for monitoring and moderating content, while respecting privacy rights and maintaining a balanced approach to online governance.

8. Encourage Digital Well-being: Promote digital well-being and responsible online behavior by advocating for strategies that encourage individuals to maintain healthy relationships with technology. Emphasize the importance of mindful online consumption, the critical evaluation of information, and the fostering of meaningful connections beyond the digital realm.

9. Stay Informed and Educate Others: Stay informed about the latest trends and tactics used in online radicalization, and educate others about the risks and challenges associated with it. Share reliable information, resources, and best practices with your social network, empowering others to navigate the online landscape safely and responsibly.

10. Support Research and Innovation: Support research and innovation in the field of countering online radicalization. Encourage collaborations between academics, experts, and policymakers to better understand the mechanisms of online radicalization and develop effective strategies for prevention and intervention.

Advocate for Human Rights

In the fight against political extremism, advocating for human rights, fairness, and justice stands as a critical strategy to prevent individuals from feeling marginalized and driven towards extremist ideologies. By promoting the principles of equality, dignity, and social justice, we create a society where everyone feels heard, valued, and included. Let's explore actionable steps that you can take to contribute to the fight against political extremism through advocating for human rights.

1. Raise Awareness: Raise awareness about human rights issues by sharing information, resources, and stories that shed light on the challenges faced by marginalized groups. Utilize social media, community events, and conversations to highlight the importance of human rights and their role in preventing extremism.

2. Support Human Rights Organizations: Support human rights organizations that work tirelessly to protect and advocate for the rights of vulnerable communities. Contribute through donations, volunteering, or raising awareness about their work, amplifying their impact and promoting a more equitable society.

3. Advocate for Policy Change: Advocate for policy changes that prioritize human rights, fairness, and justice. Engage with local and national policymakers, expressing concerns and promoting legislation that upholds the principles of equality, non-discrimination, and inclusivity.

4. Promote Diversity and Inclusion: Foster diversity and inclusion in all aspects of life, from workplaces to communities. Encourage organizations and institutions to adopt inclusive practices, policies, and hiring processes that value diversity and provide equal opportunities for all individuals.

5. Challenge Discrimination and Prejudice: Challenge discrimination and prejudice whenever encountered, whether in personal interactions, public discussions, or online spaces. Speak out against hate speech, stereotypes, and biases, promoting a culture of respect, empathy, and understanding.

6. Engage in Peaceful Protests: Engage in peaceful protests and demonstrations that advocate for human rights, social justice, and equality. Join like-minded individuals in collective action to amplify the voices of marginalized communities and raise awareness about systemic issues.

7. Educate Yourself and Others: Educate yourself and others about human rights, fairness, and justice. Stay informed about global and local human rights challenges, learn about the experiences of marginalized communities, and share this knowledge to inspire action and empathy.

8. Foster Dialogue and Understanding: Foster dialogue and understanding between diverse groups, promoting respectful conversations that challenge stereotypes and foster empathy. Engage in intergroup dialogues, community events, or initiatives that encourage open discussions on human rights issues.

9. Support Marginalized Communities: Support marginalized communities by actively seeking out their voices, concerns, and perspectives. Amplify their stories, struggles, and achievements, empowering them to take an active role in shaping policies and practices that affect their lives.

10. Lead by Example: Lead by example in upholding human rights, fairness, and justice in your own actions and interactions. Treat others with respect, challenge discriminatory behaviors, and promote inclusivity in your personal and professional life, inspiring others to follow suit.

Leverage Influencers

In the fight against political extremism, leveraging influencers and providing safe outlets for grievances become essential strategies to counter extremist ideologies and foster dialogue. Influencers and respected figures possess the power to shape public opinion and reach large audiences, making their engagement crucial in promoting alternative narratives. Furthermore, creating safe spaces for individuals to express their grievances constructively helps prevent the accumulation of frustrations that may lead to extremist inclinations. Let's explore actionable steps that you can take to contribute to the fight against political extremism.

1. Identify and Engage with Influencers: Identify influencers and respected figures who possess a broad reach and align with values that oppose extremism. Engage with them through social media, letters, or public events to raise awareness about the dangers of political extremism and encourage them to use their platforms to promote tolerance, understanding, and democratic values.

2. Support Responsible Content Creation: Support content creators and media outlets that produce responsible and informative content, challenging extremist ideologies. Share their work, engage with their content, and provide constructive feedback to encourage them to continue addressing political extremism in their narratives.

3. Foster Dialogue with Influencers: Engage in dialogue with influencers, respected figures, and thought leaders who have the potential to shape public opinion. Offer to collaborate on initiatives, provide resources, or share personal stories that illustrate the importance of countering extremism and promoting inclusive values.

4. Create Safe Spaces for Dialogue: Organize community meetings, open forums, or mediated discussions that provide safe outlets for individuals to express their grievances and frustrations. Foster an environment where diverse perspectives can be heard, respected, and constructively addressed, promoting understanding and preventing the escalation of extremist tendencies.

5. Establish Online Platforms for Constructive Discussions: Create online platforms or engage with existing ones that encourage respectful and constructive discussions around political grievances. Provide guidelines to ensure a safe and inclusive environment, moderating discussions to prevent the spread of extremist views and enabling productive dialogue.

6. Collaborate with Community Organizations: Collaborate with community organizations, non-profits, and local institutions to organize events and initiatives that address grievances and frustrations. Create opportunities for individuals to voice their concerns, propose solutions, and collaborate in finding constructive ways to address underlying issues.

7. Foster Empathy and Active Listening: Promote empathy and active listening in discussions and interactions, both online and offline. Encourage individuals to approach conversations with an open mind, seeking to understand the perspectives and experiences of others, even if they differ from their own.

8. Provide Mediation and Facilitation: Develop mediation and facilitation skills to help individuals engage in constructive dialogue. Offer support and guidance to ensure discussions remain respectful, inclusive, and productive, allowing grievances to be heard and addressed in a safe and constructive manner.

9. Collaborate with Mental Health Professionals: Collaborate with mental health professionals to provide support for individuals experiencing distress, frustration, or radicalization tendencies. Ensure access to resources, counseling, and assistance in addressing underlying psychological factors that may contribute to extremist inclinations.

10. Advocate for Policies that Address Grievances: Advocate for policies that address societal grievances and frustrations, promoting social justice, equality, and inclusive governance. Engage with policymakers, participate in public consultations, and support initiatives that aim to address the root causes of political extremism.

Develop Individual Resilience

In the fight against political extremism, developing individual resilience becomes a key strategy to counter extremist narratives and empower individuals to resist radical ideologies. By equipping individuals with life skills, mentorship opportunities, and initiatives that foster self-esteem, we can help build their capacity to critically evaluate information, navigate societal challenges, and resist the allure of extremist narratives. Let's explore actionable steps that you can take to contribute to the fight against political extremism through developing individual resilience.

1. Implement Life Skills Training: Advocate for the implementation of life skills training programs in educational institutions, community centers, and other relevant settings. These programs can provide individuals with crucial skills such as critical thinking, problem-solving, empathy, emotional regulation, and media literacy, empowering them to navigate complex societal issues and resist extremist narratives.

2. Establish Mentorship Programs: Create mentorship programs that connect individuals, especially youth, with mentors who can provide guidance, support, and positive role modeling. These relationships can foster resilience by offering valuable insights, advice, and opportunities for personal growth and development.

3. Promote Self-Esteem Building Initiatives: Support initiatives that promote self-esteem, self-confidence, and a sense of purpose among individuals. This can include workshops, seminars, or community activities that encourage personal growth, positive self-image, and a strong sense of identity, reducing vulnerability to extremist narratives.

4. Foster Critical Thinking Skills: Advocate for educational programs and initiatives that foster critical thinking skills, encouraging individuals to question and evaluate information, recognize logical fallacies, and identify manipulative tactics used by extremist ideologies. This empowers individuals to make informed judgments and resist the influence of radical narratives.

5. Encourage Media Literacy: Promote media literacy education to help individuals discern reliable information from misinformation and propaganda. Encourage critical evaluation of news sources, fact-checking, and the understanding of biases and manipulative techniques employed in media content, enabling individuals to navigate the media landscape more effectively.

6. Support Community Engagement: Encourage individuals to actively engage in their communities through volunteering, participating in civic activities, and joining community organizations. This fosters a sense of belonging, social connection, and a shared purpose, which are crucial elements in building individual resilience against extremist ideologies.

7. Encourage Dialogue and Debate: Foster an environment that encourages open dialogue, respectful debate, and the exploration of diverse perspectives. Promote platforms where individuals can engage in constructive discussions, exchange ideas, and challenge extremist narratives through reasoned arguments and evidence-based discourse.

8. Provide Resources for Mental Well-being: Advocate for accessible mental health resources and support services that address the psychological well-being of individuals. This includes promoting awareness of mental health issues, reducing stigma, and ensuring access to counseling, therapy, and support networks.

9. Nurture Positive Social Connections: Encourage the development of positive social connections and relationships, both online and offline. Promote inclusivity, empathy, and mutual understanding, fostering environments where individuals feel supported, valued, and connected to their communities.

10. Collaborate with Educational Institutions: Collaborate with educational institutions to integrate resilience-building initiatives into curricula and extracurricular activities. This can include incorporating topics related to extremism, critical thinking, media literacy, and resilience into relevant subjects, providing students with the necessary tools to resist extremist narratives.

Use Positive Messaging

In the fight against political extremism, utilizing positive messaging emerges as an essential tactic to counter extremist ideologies and promote unity, peace, and cooperation. By emphasizing the positive aspects of these values, we can inspire individuals to embrace a shared vision of a harmonious society and create an environment that is resistant to the appeal of extremist narratives. Let's explore actionable steps that you can take to contribute to the fight against political extremism through utilizing positive messaging.

1. Frame Discussions in Positive Terms: When engaging in discussions about political ideologies, focus on positive aspects such as unity, inclusivity, and shared goals. Emphasize the benefits of cooperation, understanding, and collaboration rather than solely highlighting the negatives of extremism. By reframing the conversation in positive terms, we can inspire individuals to aspire to a better future.

2. Highlight Success Stories: Share success stories that illustrate the positive outcomes of unity, peace, and cooperation. Highlight instances where diverse communities have come together to address common challenges, celebrate achievements, and promote social cohesion. These stories can serve as powerful examples of the strength and resilience that can be achieved through positive collaboration.

3. Engage in Constructive Dialogue: Encourage and participate in constructive dialogue with individuals who hold different political views. Instead of focusing on disagreements, seek common ground and opportunities for collaboration. This approach can foster understanding, bridge divides, and promote a sense of shared purpose.

4. Share Positive Examples: Utilize social media, public forums, and personal conversations to share positive examples of unity, peace, and cooperation. Highlight initiatives, projects, and individuals who exemplify these values, showcasing their contributions to a more harmonious society. By sharing these positive examples, we can inspire others to embrace similar attitudes and actions.

5. Collaborate on Positive Initiatives: Collaborate with community organizations, religious institutions, and local institutions to initiate positive projects and initiatives. These could include community service programs, interfaith dialogues, or cultural exchange events that promote understanding, tolerance, and cooperation. By actively participating in such initiatives, we demonstrate the power of positive action in shaping a more inclusive society.

6. Support Positive Media Content: Support media outlets that prioritize positive narratives, unity, and cooperation. Share and engage with content that highlights stories of hope, resilience, and collective progress. By supporting positive media content, we encourage a media landscape that counters extremist ideologies and fosters a sense of shared values.

7. Promote Interpersonal Connections: Encourage interpersonal connections and relationships among diverse individuals. Foster environments where people from different backgrounds can interact, collaborate, and build meaningful relationships. These connections contribute to breaking down barriers, dispelling stereotypes, and nurturing a sense of belonging.

8. Lead by Example: Lead by example in embodying positive values of unity, peace, and cooperation. Demonstrate kindness, empathy, and respect in your interactions with others. By consistently modeling these behaviors, you inspire those around you to adopt a similar approach and contribute to a more positive and inclusive society.

9. Foster a Culture of Appreciation: Foster a culture of appreciation and recognition for individuals and groups who promote unity, peace, and cooperation. Celebrate their efforts, acknowledge their positive impact, and inspire others to follow their lead. By amplifying and appreciating these contributions, we create a ripple effect that encourages more individuals to engage in positive actions.

10. Participate in Peace-building Activities: Engage in peace-building activities that promote unity, reconciliation, and understanding. This could involve participating in conflict resolution workshops, volunteering for organizations dedicated to peace-building, or supporting initiatives that bring together communities affected by conflict. By actively participating in these activities, we contribute to a more peaceful and cohesive society.

Fact-Checking Platforms

In the battle against political extremism, supporting fact-checking platforms becomes an essential strategy to combat the spread of misinformation and propaganda. By promoting initiatives that debunk false information and expose the manipulation tactics used by extremist ideologies, we can equip individuals with accurate knowledge and empower them to make informed decisions. Let's explore actionable steps that you can take to contribute to the fight against political extremism through supporting fact-checking platforms.

1. Spread Awareness: Raise awareness about the existence and importance of fact-checking platforms among your social circles, online communities, and local networks. Share information about reputable fact-checking organizations and encourage others to utilize these resources when evaluating news and information.

2. Verify Information Before Sharing: Before sharing news or information on social media or other platforms, take a moment to fact-check it. Use reliable fact-checking websites or apps to verify the accuracy of the content. By being diligent in our own sharing habits, we can contribute to the dissemination of truthful and reliable information.

3. Support Fact-Checking Organizations: Support fact-checking organizations by following them on social media, subscribing to their newsletters, and sharing their content. This helps amplify their reach and increases awareness of their valuable work in debunking misinformation and propaganda.

4. Volunteer or Contribute: Consider volunteering your time or contributing financially to fact-checking organizations. They often rely on the support of volunteers and donors to continue their important work. By getting involved, you can directly contribute to the fight against misinformation and extremism.

5. Educate Others: Take the initiative to educate others about the importance of fact-checking and critical thinking. Share resources, conduct workshops, or engage in conversations that promote the skills needed to evaluate information accurately. By empowering others with the tools to distinguish fact from fiction, we build a collective defense against extremist narratives.

6. Encourage Media Literacy: Advocate for media literacy education in schools and communities. Promote the integration of critical thinking, source evaluation, and fact-checking skills into educational curricula. By nurturing media literacy, we equip individuals, especially the younger generation, with the ability to navigate the complex media landscape and identify reliable information.

7. Report Disinformation: Actively report instances of disinformation or propaganda that you come across on social media platforms or other online spaces. By flagging false content, you contribute to the efforts of platform administrators and encourage responsible information dissemination.

8. Engage in Constructive Online Discussions: Participate in online discussions and comment sections with an emphasis on providing factual information and logical arguments. By actively countering misinformation and promoting evidence-based discourse, you help create a more informed and constructive online environment.

9. Encourage Critical Thinking: Encourage critical thinking among your peers and within your social networks. Promote healthy skepticism and provide resources that facilitate fact-checking and critical evaluation of information. By fostering a culture of critical thinking, we strengthen our collective resilience against extremist narratives.

Support Ex-Extremist Speakers

In the fight against political extremism, supporting ex-extremist speakers can be a powerful strategy to counter extremist ideologies. These individuals, who have firsthand experience with extremist movements, can provide unique insights and narratives that challenge the allure of radical ideologies. Let's explore actionable steps that you can take to contribute to the fight against political extremism through supporting ex-extremist speakers.

1. Seek out Ex-Extremist Speakers: Actively seek opportunities to listen to ex-extremist speakers who share their personal journeys of radicalization, disillusionment, and reintegration into society. Attend lectures, conferences, or events where these individuals are invited to speak. Engage in open-minded and empathetic listening, as their stories can provide valuable insights and alternative narratives.

2. Amplify Their Voices: Share the messages and stories of ex-extremist speakers through your personal and online networks. Utilize social media platforms, blogs, or community forums to disseminate their perspectives and experiences. By amplifying their voices, you contribute to a broader awareness of the detrimental effects of extremism and the potential for redemption and positive change.

3. Support Organizations: Support organizations that provide platforms for ex-extremist speakers to share their stories. These organizations often organize events, workshops, and outreach programs that aim to educate communities about the dangers of extremism and promote dialogue and understanding. Donate your time, resources, or expertise to help these organizations in their mission.

4. Foster Dialogue and Reflection: Engage in constructive dialogue and reflection after listening to ex-extremist speakers. Discuss their narratives with friends, family, or colleagues, encouraging critical thinking and exploring the factors that contribute to radicalization. By fostering open and respectful conversations, we deepen our understanding and collective resilience against extremist ideologies.

5. Educate Others: Share the insights gained from ex-extremist speakers with others, particularly young individuals who may be vulnerable to radicalization. Use their stories as educational tools to raise awareness, promote critical thinking, and empower individuals to resist the pull of extremism. Collaborate with educational institutions or community organizations to integrate these narratives into educational programs.

6. Advocate for Ex-Extremist Programs: Advocate for the development of programs and initiatives that support the rehabilitation and reintegration of individuals who have left extremist movements. These programs can provide counseling, mentorship, vocational training, and social support, helping ex-extremists rebuild their lives and become agents of positive change in their communities.

7. Encourage Empathy and Understanding: Foster empathy and understanding towards individuals who have disengaged from extremist ideologies. Encourage others to approach these individuals with compassion and provide opportunities for them to share their experiences. By facilitating empathy and understanding, we promote the acceptance of former extremists into society and reduce the likelihood of their re-radicalization.

8. Challenge Stigmatization: Challenge the stigmatization and marginalization of ex-extremists in society. Advocate for policies that promote their reintegration and counter societal biases that hinder their ability to rebuild their lives. By creating an environment of acceptance and support, we contribute to the prevention of extremist recidivism and promote a more inclusive society.

9. Support Research and Scholarly Efforts: Support research and scholarly efforts that aim to understand the complexities of radicalization, disengagement, and rehabilitation. By backing academic studies, you contribute to the knowledge base on extremism and provide insights that can inform preventive strategies and interventions.

10. Engage in Self-Reflection: Engage in self-reflection and examine your own biases and preconceptions. Explore how societal factors contribute to the appeal of extremist ideologies and consider ways to counter those factors in your own life. By cultivating self-awareness and a willingness to challenge our own beliefs, we set an example for others and contribute to a culture of open-mindedness and critical thinking.

Promote Shared Interests

In the fight against political extremism, promoting shared interests becomes a vital strategy to bridge divides and foster understanding among individuals with different political ideologies. By identifying common activities or goals that transcend political boundaries, we create opportunities for people to come together, engage in meaningful interactions, and find areas of agreement. Let's explore actionable steps that you can take to contribute to the fight against political extremism through promoting shared interests.

1. Organize Collaborative Projects: Initiate collaborative projects or initiatives that bring together individuals from diverse political backgrounds. These projects could focus on community development, environmental conservation, social welfare, or any other cause that aligns with shared values. By working towards a common goal, people can discover commonalities and build relationships that transcend their political differences.

2. Participate in Interfaith or Interpolitical Dialogue: Engage in interfaith or interpolitical dialogue to foster understanding and cooperation. Attend community events, discussion forums, or workshops that encourage respectful conversations and the exploration of different perspectives. By actively listening to others and seeking areas of agreement, we can find common ground and establish stronger bonds across political divides.

3. Support Bipartisan Initiatives: Advocate for and support bipartisan initiatives that address pressing social issues. Collaborate with individuals from different political ideologies to promote policies and actions that bridge gaps and prioritize the common good. By focusing on shared interests and common values, we can transcend partisan divisions and work towards meaningful solutions.

4. Foster Social Connections: Actively foster social connections with individuals from different political backgrounds. Engage in social activities, community events, or volunteer work where people from diverse ideologies come together. By building personal relationships, we create opportunities for understanding, empathy, and respectful dialogue.

5. Promote Civil Discourse: Encourage civil discourse and respectful communication in personal interactions, online discussions, and public forums. Model constructive dialogue by listening attentively, expressing opinions respectfully, and seeking common ground. By promoting a culture of civil discourse, we create an environment that encourages understanding and cooperation across political divides.

6. Bridge Divides through Arts and Culture: Utilize arts and cultural activities to bridge political divides. Support artistic events, exhibitions, or performances that promote dialogue, understanding, and appreciation of different perspectives. By leveraging the power of art, we can create spaces for empathy, reflection, and connection.

7. Encourage Political Diversity: Advocate for political diversity in various spheres, including workplaces, academic institutions, and social organizations. Embrace the value of diverse viewpoints and challenge echo chambers by fostering environments that encourage a range of political opinions. By exposing ourselves to diverse perspectives, we broaden our understanding and promote inclusive dialogue.

8. Collaborate on Local Issues: Collaborate with individuals from different political backgrounds on local issues that directly impact the community. Attend local government meetings, join community organizations, or volunteer for neighborhood projects. By focusing on shared interests and working towards common goals, we demonstrate that cooperation and understanding transcend political ideologies.

9. Support Cross-Ideological Media: Support media platforms and outlets that prioritize cross-ideological discussions and provide balanced coverage of political issues. Consume news from diverse sources and seek out perspectives that challenge your own beliefs. By diversifying our media consumption, we gain a more comprehensive understanding of different viewpoints and foster a healthier discourse.

10. Lead by Example: Lead by example in promoting shared interests and fostering understanding among individuals with different political ideologies. Demonstrate empathy, respect, and openness in your interactions. By embodying these values, we inspire others to do the same and contribute to a more inclusive and cooperative society.

Foster Inter-Generational Dialogue

In the fight against political extremism, fostering inter-generational dialogue evolves into a vital approach to bridge gaps and promote understanding among individuals of different age groups. By facilitating conversations between generations, we create opportunities to address misconceptions, challenge stereotypes, and build bridges of empathy and understanding. Drawing inspiration from renowned thinkers who emphasize the importance of dialogue and mutual respect, let's explore actionable steps that you can take to contribute to the fight against political extremism through fostering inter-generational dialogue.

1. Create Intergenerational Spaces: Establish spaces where individuals from different age groups can come together and engage in meaningful conversations. These spaces could include community centers, educational institutions, or local events that encourage inter-generational interactions. By providing platforms for dialogue, we foster understanding and bridge generational divides.

2. Organize Intergenerational Activities: Organize activities that bring together people from different generations to collaborate on projects, share experiences, and learn from one another. This could involve workshops, mentorship programs, or community initiatives that encourage inter-generational exchange. By actively participating in these activities, we break down barriers and build connections based on shared goals and experiences.

3. Facilitate Intergenerational Dialogue: Act as a facilitator or mediator in inter-generational discussions. Create safe and respectful environments where individuals from different age groups can express their thoughts, concerns, and perspectives. Encourage active listening, empathy, and open-mindedness, fostering mutual understanding and dispelling misconceptions.

4. Embrace Technology as a Tool: Utilize technology as a tool to connect generations and facilitate dialogue. Encourage the use of social media platforms, online forums, or video conferencing to engage in inter-generational conversations. By leveraging technology, we overcome physical barriers and create spaces for diverse voices to be heard.

5. Promote Intergenerational Mentorship: Encourage inter-generational mentorship programs where younger individuals can benefit from the wisdom and guidance of older generations, while older individuals gain new perspectives and insights from younger generations. By fostering mentorship relationships, we facilitate mutual learning and understanding.

6. Share Stories and Experiences: Encourage individuals from different generations to share their stories and experiences, allowing for a deeper understanding of the challenges, triumphs, and perspectives that shape their lives. By actively listening to each other's narratives, we cultivate empathy and bridge the gap between generations.

7. Bridge the Digital Divide: Take steps to bridge the digital divide between generations by providing access to digital resources and offering technology training for older individuals. By empowering older generations with digital literacy skills, we enable them to participate fully in the digital age and engage in online dialogues with younger generations.

8. Foster Intergenerational Learning: Promote inter-generational learning opportunities where individuals from different age groups can come together to learn new skills, explore shared interests, and engage in collaborative projects. By fostering inter-generational learning, we create spaces for meaningful interactions and the exchange of knowledge and perspectives.

9. Advocate for Intergenerational Policies: Advocate for policies that prioritize inter-generational cooperation, representation, and decision-making. Support initiatives that involve different age groups in policymaking processes and ensure that the concerns and perspectives of all generations are taken into account. By advocating for inter-generational policies, we promote inclusivity and strengthen the bonds between generations.

10. Lead by Example: Lead by example in fostering inter-generational dialogue and understanding. Engage in respectful and meaningful conversations with individuals from different age groups, demonstrate empathy, and challenge age-based stereotypes. By embracing inter-generational connections, we inspire others to do the same and contribute to a society that values the wisdom and contributions of all generations.

Address Discrimination

In the fight against political extremism, addressing discrimination gains prominence as a critical method to create a more inclusive and equitable society. Discrimination in any form can contribute to feelings of marginalization, resentment, and disillusionment, which can potentially lead individuals towards extremist ideologies. Let's explore actionable steps that you can take to contribute to the fight against political extremism through addressing discrimination.

1. Educate Yourself: Take the initiative to educate yourself about various forms of discrimination, including racial, ethnic, religious, gender-based, or any other form of marginalization. Read books, attend workshops, and engage in conversations that deepen your understanding of the issues and experiences faced by marginalized communities.

2. Challenge Bias: Examine your own biases and prejudices and actively work to challenge them. Reflect on your thoughts, attitudes, and actions, and strive to treat all individuals with fairness, respect, and dignity. Engage in self-reflection and dialogue to uncover and dismantle unconscious biases.

3. Speak Up: Speak up against discrimination when you witness it in your personal life, at work, or in public spaces. Use your voice to advocate for equal rights, justice, and inclusivity. By standing up against discrimination, you create a safer and more supportive environment for all individuals.

4. Support Anti-Discrimination Organizations: Support organizations that work towards combating discrimination and promoting equality. Donate to or volunteer with local or national initiatives that actively address systemic biases and advocate for the rights of marginalized communities. Your contribution can make a significant impact in the fight against discrimination.

5. Foster Empathy: Cultivate empathy by seeking to understand and validate the experiences of those who have been marginalized or discriminated against. Engage in conversations with empathy and compassion, and actively listen to the stories and perspectives of individuals from different backgrounds.

6. Take Action Against Systemic Discrimination: Get involved in efforts to address systemic discrimination by supporting initiatives that advocate for policy changes and systemic reforms. Join campaigns, sign petitions, and engage in peaceful activism that aims to dismantle structures that perpetuate discrimination.

7. Be an Ally: Be an ally to marginalized communities by supporting and amplifying their voices. Learn about the challenges they face, listen to their experiences, and actively work to dismantle barriers that impede their progress. Stand in solidarity with marginalized groups and use your privilege to advocate for justice and equality.

8. Engage in Difficult Conversations: Engage in respectful and constructive conversations about discrimination and its impact. Initiate dialogues with friends, family members, colleagues, or acquaintances to promote understanding and challenge misconceptions. Foster an environment where open and honest discussions about discrimination can take place.

9. Lead by Example: Lead by example in addressing discrimination by embodying values of inclusivity, respect, and equality in your daily interactions. Model behavior that encourages empathy, fairness, and justice. By leading through your actions, you inspire others to follow suit and contribute to a society that rejects discrimination and embraces diversity.

Counter Hate Speech

In the fight against political extremism, countering hate speech turns into an indispensable technique to foster a more tolerant and inclusive society. Hate speech, whether expressed online or offline, can fuel division, animosity, and extremist ideologies. Let's explore actionable steps that you can take to contribute to the fight against political extremism through countering hate speech.

1. Promote Civil Discourse: Foster an environment of civil discourse in your personal interactions and online engagements. Engage in respectful conversations, listen to differing viewpoints, and respond with empathy and understanding. By modeling civil discourse, you contribute to a culture that values dialogue over hostility.

2. Report Hate Speech: Actively report instances of hate speech encountered online or offline through appropriate channels. Social media platforms, online forums, and local authorities may provide mechanisms to report and address hate speech. By reporting, you contribute to the prevention and moderation of harmful content.

3. Educate Others: Share accurate information and resources to educate others about the harmful effects of hate speech. Communicate the importance of respectful dialogue, empathy, and the potential consequences of hate speech in perpetuating division and extremism. Raise awareness among friends, family, and community members about the impact of hate speech on individuals and society.

4. Support Anti-Hate Organizations: Support organizations and initiatives dedicated to countering hate speech. Contribute financially, volunteer your time, or participate in their campaigns and events. These organizations work towards monitoring, combating, and raising awareness about hate speech, promoting tolerance and inclusivity.

5. Foster Online Communities of Respect: Actively engage in online communities that promote respectful and inclusive discussions. Contribute positively, challenge hateful narratives, and support those who advocate for a culture of respect and understanding. Encourage online platforms to establish and enforce policies against hate speech.

6. Engage in Counter-Speech: Respond to instances of hate speech with constructive counter-speech. Articulate opposing viewpoints, challenge misinformation, and promote empathy and understanding. By countering hateful narratives with thoughtful and persuasive arguments, you contribute to fostering more inclusive and tolerant conversations.

7. Promote Media Literacy: Develop media literacy skills to discern between reliable information and hateful propaganda. Educate yourself about the techniques used to spread hate speech and misinformation. Share this knowledge with others to empower them in navigating and critically analyzing media sources.

8. Support Hate Crime Reporting: Encourage the reporting of hate crimes and support victims who experience hate-based incidents. Collaborate with local authorities, community organizations, and victim support networks to ensure that incidents of hate are properly documented, investigated, and addressed.

9. Encourage Dialogue and Understanding: Encourage dialogue and understanding between different communities, fostering empathy and breaking down stereotypes. Actively participate in interfaith, intercultural, and intergroup initiatives that promote collaboration, cooperation, and mutual respect.

10. Lead by Example: Lead by example in your own language and behavior. Avoid engaging in hate speech, derogatory language, or dehumanizing narratives. Model respect, empathy, and tolerance in your interactions with others, inspiring those around you to follow suit.

Emphasize Common Goals

In the pursuit of combating political extremism, emphasizing common goals becomes a vital approach to fostering cooperation and unity across political and ideological lines. By recognizing shared interests and aspirations, we can bridge divides and create a sense of collective purpose that transcends divisive narratives. Let's explore actionable steps that you can take to contribute to the fight against political extremism by emphasizing common goals.

1. Seek Common Ground: Actively seek out common ground with individuals who hold different political or ideological beliefs. Engage in conversations that focus on shared aspirations, values, and concerns rather than dwelling on divisive issues. By emphasizing commonalities, we can build bridges of understanding and collaboration.

2. Collaborate on Community Projects: Participate in community projects and initiatives that bring people together around shared goals. This could involve volunteering for causes such as environmental conservation, poverty alleviation, education, or any other endeavor that fosters cooperation and promotes the well-being of the community. By working side by side towards common objectives, we build relationships and break down ideological barriers.

3. Promote Dialogue and Listening: Encourage open dialogue and active listening among individuals with diverse perspectives. Create spaces where people feel comfortable sharing their thoughts and experiences, and foster an environment where different viewpoints are respected and understood. By engaging in meaningful conversations, we can broaden our understanding and discover shared goals that unite us.

4. Advocate for Bipartisanship: Advocate for bipartisanship and cross-party cooperation in political discourse. Support politicians and leaders who prioritize collaboration and finding common ground, rather than perpetuating polarizing rhetoric. By promoting a politics of cooperation, we can bridge ideological gaps and foster a more inclusive and productive political environment.

5. Engage in Grassroots Movements: Get involved in grassroots movements that prioritize common goals and interests. Join organizations or campaigns that seek to address issues that transcend political boundaries, such as climate change, social justice, or economic inequality. By working together towards these shared objectives, we can foster a sense of unity and solidarity.

6. Encourage Cross-Ideological Dialogue: Encourage and facilitate cross-ideological dialogue and discussions. Organize events, panels, or forums where individuals from different political backgrounds can come together to exchange ideas and perspectives in a respectful and constructive manner. By promoting dialogue, we can foster mutual understanding and break down stereotypes.

7. Amplify Voices of Unity: Use your platform, whether it be social media, community gatherings, or personal networks, to amplify voices of unity and cooperation. Share stories, articles, or speeches that emphasize shared goals and the importance of working together across ideological lines. By highlighting these narratives, we can counteract divisive rhetoric and inspire others to embrace common goals.

8. Support Coalition-Building Initiatives: Support coalition-building initiatives that aim to bring diverse groups and organizations together around shared interests. Contribute your time, resources, or expertise to facilitate collaboration and cooperation among different stakeholders. By strengthening alliances and fostering joint efforts, we can maximize our impact in promoting common goals.

9. Foster Interdisciplinary Collaboration: Encourage interdisciplinary collaboration in various fields, such as academia, arts, and business. Support initiatives that bring together individuals from different disciplines to tackle complex problems and find innovative solutions. By fostering collaboration across disciplines, we can tap into diverse perspectives and enhance our collective ability to address societal challenges.

10. Lead by Example: Lead by example in emphasizing common goals and promoting cooperation. Demonstrate through your actions and words the importance of transcending political divides and working towards shared objectives. By embodying unity and cooperation, we inspire others to do the same.

Empower Voices of Moderation

In the fight against political extremism, empowering voices of moderation is a critical strategy to promote balanced and constructive dialogue. These voices act as a counterbalance to extreme ideologies and contribute to a more nuanced and inclusive public discourse. Let's explore actionable steps that you can take to contribute to the fight against political extremism by empowering voices of moderation.

1. Seek Out Moderate Perspectives: Actively seek out and engage with moderate perspectives from various political and ideological groups. Explore different sources of information, listen to podcasts or read articles that present balanced viewpoints. By exposing ourselves to diverse perspectives, we broaden our understanding and contribute to a more informed and nuanced dialogue.

2. Share Moderating Content: Share articles, speeches, or social media posts that promote moderation, reason, and constructive dialogue. Amplify voices that emphasize the importance of listening, empathy, and finding common ground. By sharing this content, we contribute to a more balanced and inclusive narrative in public discourse.

3. Foster Civil Discourse: Encourage civil discourse and respectful dialogue in your own interactions, whether online or offline. Avoid inflammatory language or personal attacks and instead focus on understanding different perspectives and finding areas of agreement. By modeling civil discourse, we set an example for others and contribute to a culture of respectful engagement.

4. Engage in Bridge-Building Conversations: Initiate conversations with individuals who hold different political or ideological views, seeking common ground and areas of agreement. Emphasize shared values and goals, and listen actively to their perspectives. By engaging in bridge-building conversations, we foster understanding and build connections that transcend ideological differences.

5. Support Moderate Voices: Support and promote moderate voices within your social circles, online platforms, and community. Attend events or webinars where moderates share their insights and experiences. By actively supporting and elevating moderate voices, we create space for more balanced and constructive dialogue.

6. Encourage Bipartisan Collaboration: Advocate for bipartisan collaboration and cooperation among political representatives and leaders. Support politicians who prioritize finding common ground and working across party lines. By encouraging bipartisanship, we promote moderation and compromise as essential elements of democratic governance.

7. Educate Others on Moderation: Share educational resources and materials that highlight the importance of moderation in political discourse. Organize discussions or workshops that explore the value of balanced perspectives and constructive dialogue. By educating others on the benefits of moderation, we foster a greater appreciation for diverse viewpoints and promote a more inclusive political landscape.

8. Counter Extreme Narratives: Challenge and counter extreme narratives by providing alternative viewpoints and evidence-based arguments. Engage respectfully with individuals espousing extremist views, offering a reasoned and moderate perspective. By countering extreme narratives, we contribute to a more balanced and informed public discourse.

9. Foster Empathy and Understanding: Cultivate empathy and understanding towards individuals who hold different political beliefs or ideologies. Seek to understand their motivations and experiences, even if you disagree with their views. By fostering empathy, we create space for respectful dialogue and bridge ideological divides.

Create Open Dialogues

In the fight against political extremism, creating open dialogues serves as a powerful tool to raise awareness, promote understanding, and combat the dangers associated with extremist ideologies. Let's explore actionable steps that you can take to contribute to this strategy and help fight political extremism.

1. Initiate Conversations: Take the initiative to start conversations about extremism in various settings, including public spaces, schools, and online platforms. Create a safe and inclusive environment where individuals can openly discuss their concerns, share perspectives, and learn from one another.

2. Foster Active Listening: Practice active listening during these dialogues, showing genuine interest and respect for different viewpoints. Allow individuals to express their thoughts and feelings without judgment or interruption. By fostering active listening, we create space for empathy and understanding to flourish.

3. Encourage Diverse Perspectives: Encourage the participation of individuals with diverse backgrounds, beliefs, and experiences in these open dialogues. Promote an inclusive environment that welcomes a range of perspectives to foster a comprehensive understanding of the complexities surrounding political extremism.

4. Provide Education and Resources: Share educational resources, such as articles, documentaries, or books, that provide insights into the origins, consequences, and tactics of extremist ideologies. Equip participants with knowledge to engage in informed discussions and develop a deeper understanding of the subject matter.

5. Engage Youth and Students: Collaborate with educational institutions and community organizations to create open dialogues about extremism specifically tailored for youth and students. Offer age-appropriate discussions that encourage critical thinking, empathy, and resilience against extremist ideologies.

6. Utilize Online Platforms: Utilize online platforms to facilitate open dialogues about extremism. Participate in online forums, social media discussions, or dedicated platforms that promote respectful and constructive conversations on the topic. Leverage technology to reach a broader audience and foster a global exchange of ideas.

7. Provide Facilitation and Mediation: Offer facilitation and mediation skills to ensure that these open dialogues remain productive and respectful. Foster an environment where participants feel comfortable expressing their views while maintaining a focus on constructive engagement. Skilled facilitators can guide discussions and ensure that all voices are heard.

8. Partner with Community Organizations: Collaborate with community organizations, nonprofits, and grassroots initiatives that work towards promoting open dialogues and combating extremism. Pool resources, share knowledge, and amplify collective efforts to foster a widespread and sustained impact.

9. Support Peer-to-Peer Initiatives: Encourage peer-to-peer initiatives where individuals can engage in open dialogues about extremism among their peers. Empower young leaders and community members to organize and facilitate these discussions, creating spaces where trust, respect, and learning can flourish.

10. Promote Follow-Up Actions: Encourage participants in open dialogues to translate their discussions into tangible actions. Foster a sense of responsibility and empower individuals to actively combat extremism within their communities. Support and promote follow-up initiatives, such as community projects, awareness campaigns, or advocacy efforts.

Endorse Ethical Journalism

In the battle against political extremism, endorsing ethical journalism plays a crucial role in countering propaganda and misinformation. Let's explore actionable steps that you can take to contribute to this strategy and help fight political extremism.

1. Seek Reliable News Sources: Actively seek out and rely on reputable news sources that adhere to ethical journalistic practices. Look for publications that prioritize fact-checking, verification of sources, and unbiased reporting. By consuming reliable news, we equip ourselves with accurate information to counteract extremist narratives.

2. Share Verified Information: When sharing news or information on social media or other platforms, ensure that it comes from credible sources. Verify the accuracy of the information before sharing to prevent the spread of false or misleading content. By being responsible sharers, we contribute to a more informed public discourse.

3. Support Independent Journalism: Support independent journalism outlets that prioritize investigative reporting and unbiased coverage. Consider subscribing to or financially supporting these outlets to sustain their efforts in delivering quality journalism. By supporting independent journalism, we uphold the importance of diverse perspectives and objective reporting.

4. Engage in Media Literacy: Educate ourselves and others about media literacy to develop critical thinking skills. Learn how to identify bias, evaluate sources, and discern reliable information from misinformation. By becoming media-literate, we become better equipped to navigate the complex media landscape and combat the influence of extremist propaganda.

5. Fact-Check and Verify: Take the initiative to fact-check information before accepting it as true. Utilize fact-checking organizations or online tools to verify claims, especially those that seem inflammatory or designed to provoke extreme reactions. By fact-checking, we promote a culture of truth-seeking and undermine the spread of false narratives.

6. Encourage Journalistic Integrity: Publicly support and commend journalists who demonstrate integrity, impartiality, and ethical reporting. Write letters of appreciation or engage in online discussions to recognize their contributions. By endorsing ethical journalism, we encourage responsible reporting and hold media organizations accountable.

7. Report Misinformation: Actively report misinformation or extremist content encountered online to relevant platforms or authorities. By reporting such content, we help reduce its visibility and limit its potential to spread and influence others. Reporting is an essential step in combating the dissemination of extremist ideologies.

8. Engage in Constructive Criticism: Engage in constructive criticism of media organizations or individual journalists when warranted. Provide feedback on biased reporting, misinformation, or sensationalism, highlighting the importance of ethical standards in journalism. By offering constructive criticism, we contribute to a culture of accountability and improvement within the media landscape.

9. Support Media Literacy Education: Advocate for media literacy education in schools and communities.

Support initiatives that provide resources, workshops, or programs aimed at equipping individuals with the skills to navigate the media landscape critically. By promoting media literacy education, we empower individuals to become discerning consumers of information.

10. Be an Informed Consumer: Take an active role in seeking diverse perspectives, fact-checking, and maintaining an open mind. Challenge our own biases and assumptions, and strive to understand different viewpoints. By being informed consumers of media, we resist the influence of extremist narratives and foster a more inclusive and informed society.

Fight Against Social Isolation

In the pursuit of combating political extremism, addressing social isolation is a vital step in creating a sense of belonging and resilience within individuals. Let's explore actionable steps that you can take to contribute to this strategy and fight against political extremism.

1. Foster Community Engagement: Actively engage in community activities and organizations that promote social interaction, inclusivity, and a sense of belonging. Participate in local events, volunteer initiatives, or neighborhood gatherings to foster meaningful connections and build strong social networks.

2. Support Mental Health Services: Advocate for and support accessible mental health services that address the underlying factors contributing to social isolation. Promote awareness of mental health resources, reduce stigma, and ensure individuals have access to the support they need to combat feelings of isolation.

3. Create Supportive Spaces: Establish safe and inclusive spaces within communities where individuals can come together, share experiences, and build relationships. Encourage the creation of support groups, discussion circles, or social clubs that provide opportunities for people to connect and form meaningful connections.

4. Encourage Interpersonal Connections: Foster interpersonal connections by encouraging open and empathetic communication. Encourage individuals to reach out to others, engage in meaningful conversations, and listen attentively to create deeper connections and combat social isolation.

5. Embrace Diversity and Inclusion: Celebrate diversity and promote inclusivity within communities. Foster an environment that respects and appreciates different cultures, backgrounds, and perspectives. By embracing diversity, we create spaces where individuals feel valued, accepted, and connected to others.

6. Strengthen Family and Community Bonds: Encourage strong family ties and community bonds by supporting initiatives that bring families and communities together. Facilitate opportunities for intergenerational connections, mentorship programs, or community events that foster a sense of belonging and support.

7. Leverage Technology for Connection: Utilize technology to bridge gaps and connect with others, especially during times of physical distancing. Encourage the use of online platforms, social media groups, or virtual communities to maintain social connections and combat isolation.

8. Promote Active Listening and Empathy: Practice active listening and empathy in our interactions with others. Seek to understand the experiences and challenges faced by individuals who may feel isolated. By demonstrating empathy, we foster a supportive environment where people feel heard, valued, and connected.

9. Advocate for Social Policies: Advocate for social policies that address the root causes of social isolation, such as affordable housing, quality education, and access to healthcare. Support initiatives that promote social integration, reduce inequality, and create opportunities for meaningful connections.

10. Educate and Raise Awareness: Educate ourselves and others about the impact of social isolation and its connection to extremist recruitment. Raise awareness through conversations, workshops, or educational campaigns to highlight the importance of social connection and combat the factors that contribute to isolation.

Dismantle Echo Chambers

In the pursuit of countering political extremism, the dismantling of echo chambers plays a crucial role in fostering open dialogue and promoting a diverse exchange of ideas. Let's explore actionable steps that you can take to contribute to this strategy and fight against political extremism.

1. Seek Diverse Perspectives: Actively seek out and engage with diverse perspectives, opinions, and sources of information. Challenge yourself to explore viewpoints that differ from your own, expanding your understanding of complex issues and fostering a more nuanced perspective.

2. Engage in Constructive Debates: Encourage and participate in constructive debates that promote respectful discourse and critical thinking. Engage in conversations with individuals from different political and ideological backgrounds, focusing on understanding their viewpoints rather than aiming to win arguments.

3. Foster Empathy and Understanding: Cultivate empathy and understanding by actively listening to others, seeking to comprehend their experiences, and considering the factors that shape their perspectives. Recognize that diverse viewpoints contribute to the richness of public discourse and provide opportunities for growth.

4. Fact-Check and Verify Information: Take the responsibility to fact-check and verify information before sharing it. Promote a culture of critical evaluation of news articles, social media posts, and other sources of information to prevent the spread of misinformation and the reinforcement of echo chambers.

5. Encourage Civil Dialogue Online: Engage in online discussions and social media platforms with civility and respect. Encourage others to express their opinions and engage in thoughtful conversations, avoiding personal attacks and inflammatory language that perpetuate echo chambers.

6. Support Media Literacy Education: Advocate for and support media literacy education in schools and communities. Promote critical thinking skills and the ability to discern reliable sources of information from misinformation and propaganda.

7. Participate in Cross-Ideological Initiatives: Engage in cross-ideological initiatives and organizations that aim to bridge gaps and foster understanding between different political and ideological groups. Support efforts that promote collaboration and cooperative problem-solving across divides.

8. Encourage Intellectual Humility: Cultivate intellectual humility by recognizing the limitations of one's own knowledge and being open to learning from others. Embrace the idea that no single perspective holds a monopoly on truth and that collective understanding is achieved through respectful dialogue.

9. Lead by Example: Serve as a role model by engaging in respectful and inclusive dialogue. Demonstrate the value of intellectual diversity and open-mindedness in your own interactions, inspiring others to follow suit.

Conclusion

As we reach the end of this exploration, it's crucial to remember that our journey is only beginning. The path we've embarked upon isn't a straight, predictable one, but rather a winding trail filled with unexpected twists and unforeseen obstacles. Yet, it's a trail we must traverse, for it leads us towards a society that is more balanced, more inclusive, and ultimately more democratic.

The fringes of our political landscape, as we've discovered, do not encapsulate our identity. They are merely the outer edges of a much larger, intricate tapestry. This tapestry is woven from countless threads, each representing a unique perspective, a distinct voice, a singular experience. It's this rich diversity that lends our democracy its strength, its resilience, and its capacity for evolution and transformation.

We've delved into the perils of extremism, the traps of "both side-isms", and the necessity of introspection and critique within our own circles. We've learned to embrace a multitude of viewpoints, to question our own biases, and to engage with ideologies that may diverge from our own. This isn't a simple task, but it's an essential one. It's through this process of exploration and understanding that we can aspire to cultivate a more balanced and equitable political discourse.

Within these pages, you've encountered hundreds of actionable steps, tangible measures that you can implement to effect change. These aren't merely theoretical suggestions, but practical tools for progress, for transformation, for the reconstruction of the democracy we cherish. Utilize them. Disseminate them. Encourage others to follow suit.

Our journey may be arduous, and the road may be winding, but we are not solitary travelers. We journey together, bound by our shared commitment to democracy, to fairness, to understanding. As we forge ahead, let's remember that it's not the destination that holds the most value, but the journey itself, the lessons we glean along the way, the transformations we effect, the lives we impact.

Together, we've initiated the process of salvaging and rebuilding our democracy. But this is merely the commencement. The road extends before us, beckoning us to continue our journey, to discover new ideas, to challenge antiquated assumptions, to construct a better, more inclusive future. Let's accept this invitation with open hearts and open minds, for together, we can shape a world that isn't defined by its extremes, but by its capacity for understanding, for empathy, for change.

So, as we turn the final page of this book, let's not perceive it as a conclusion, but as an inauguration. An inauguration of a journey that we will undertake together, a journey towards a more balanced, more inclusive, and more democratic society. A journey that commences now.

About the Author

Thomas T. Taylor is a man of many titles. In his hometown, he's known as "Mr. Friendly," a testament to his warm demeanor and unwavering dedication to his community. In the realm of academia, he's a scholar with a rich background in social psychology and political science. In the political sphere, he's a seasoned veteran, having immersed himself in local politics since his early twenties.

Taylor's journey into politics was not a career choice, but a calling. His early involvement in the political scene has given him an intimate understanding of the inner workings of governance and the pivotal role of community engagement. His approachability and commitment to his constituents have not only earned him the nickname "Mr. Friendly" but also the respect and trust of his community.

Complementing his political endeavors, Taylor's academic pursuits in social psychology and political science have provided him with a profound understanding of the societal dynamics that underpin politics. He seamlessly bridges the gap between theoretical knowledge and practical application, leveraging his academic insights to foster a more inclusive and balanced political environment.

Away from the public eye, Taylor leads a fulfilling family life. He is a loving husband and a doting father to six children. His family serves as a constant reminder of the real-world impact of political decisions, reinforcing the importance of building a society that values fairness, compassion, and understanding.

In his book, "Rebuilding Democracy: Strategies for Countering Political Extremism", Taylor brings together his wealth of political experience, academic expertise, and personal reflections. He offers a comprehensive guide to understanding and countering political extremism, hoping to inspire readers to renew their commitment to democratic values and to actively contribute to a more inclusive and balanced political discourse.

Appendix

Recommend Reading List

- "The Anatomy of Fascism" by Robert O. Paxton

- "Logically Fallacious" by Bo Bennett, PhD

- "The Authoritarian Dynamic" by Karen Stenner

- "The Righteous Mind: Why Good People Are Divided by Politics and Religion" by Jonathan Haidt

- "Uncivil Agreement: How Politics Became Our Identity" by Lilliana Mason

- "Democracy and the Human Condition" by Philip J. Ethington

- "Antifragile: Things That Gain from Disorder" by Nassim Nicholas Taleb

- "The Death of Expertise: The Campaign against Established Knowledge and Why It Matters" by Tom Nichols

- "The Road to Unfreedom: Russia, Europe, America" by Timothy Snyder

- "The Extremist Mindset: A Guide to Understanding Radicalization" by V. Tamara Russell

- "The Open Society and Its Enemies" by Karl Popper

- "Identity: The Demand for Dignity and the Politics of Resentment" by Francis Fukuyama

- "The Ideological Origins of the American Revolution" by Bernard Bailyn

- "The Better Angels of Our Nature: Why Violence Has Declined" by Steven Pinker

- "Political Tribes: Group Instinct and the Fate of Nations" by Amy Chua

- "The Power of Others: Peer Pressure, Groupthink, and How the People Around Us Shape Everything We Do" by Michael Bond

Glossary of Terms

Anti-Globalization: A movement or ideology that opposes globalization, often highlighting concerns about its impact on local economies, cultures, or sovereignty.

Antisemitism: Prejudice, discrimination, or hostility towards Jewish individuals or communities, often based on stereotypes or conspiracy theories.

Authoritarianism: A political system characterized by strong central power, limited individual freedoms, and the suppression of dissent.

Cognitive Bias: Systematic patterns of deviation from rational judgment or decision-making, often influenced by personal experiences, emotions, or preconceived notions.

Communism: A political ideology advocating for the abolition of private property, a classless society, and the collective ownership of means of production.

Conspiracy Theory: An explanation or belief that attributes significant events or phenomena to secret plots or schemes by powerful individuals or groups.

Counterterrorism: Strategies and actions aimed at preventing, deterring, and responding to terrorist activities and organizations.

Cult of Personality: A situation in which a leader or political figure is elevated to an exaggerated and worshipful status, often suppressing dissent and critical thinking.

Cyber Warfare: The use of technology, such as hacking, for political or ideological purposes to disrupt or damage computer networks, infrastructure, or information systems.

Dehumanization: The process of portraying individuals or groups as less than human, often as a means to justify violence or discrimination against them.

Dogmatism: The adherence to a set of beliefs or ideologies without question or consideration of alternative perspectives.

Echo Chamber: A situation in which individuals are exposed only to information or opinions that reinforce their existing beliefs, creating a self-reinforcing cycle of thought.

Extremist Propaganda: Material disseminated to promote radical political ideologies and recruit individuals to extremist causes.

Extremist Recruitment: The process by which individuals are targeted and persuaded to join extremist groups or adopt radical ideologies.

Fascism: An authoritarian and nationalistic political ideology that seeks to create a centralized autocratic government, suppressing dissent and emphasizing the importance of the nation or race.

Foreign Interference: The intentional involvement of external actors, such as foreign governments or organizations, in the political affairs of another country to influence outcomes.

Groupthink: A phenomenon in which the desire for conformity and consensus within a group overrides critical thinking and independent judgment.

Hate Speech: Public expression that promotes or incites violence, discrimination, or hostility towards individuals or groups based on attributes such as race, religion, or sexual orientation.

Identity Politics: The political mobilization and organization based on specific social identities, such as race, gender, or religion, often emphasizing grievances and demands for rights.

Indoctrination: The process of forcibly or systematically imparting specific beliefs, values, or ideologies, often without critical thinking or questioning.

Islamism: A political ideology that seeks to establish Islamic law (Sharia) as the foundation of governance, often associated with the politicization of Islam.

Lone Wolf Terrorism: Acts of terrorism carried out by individuals who act independently, often without direct guidance or support from a larger organization.

Nationalism: A strong sense of loyalty and devotion to one's nation, often accompanied by the belief in its superiority over other nations.

Paramilitary Groups: Organized armed groups that operate outside the formal military structure, often characterized by extremist ideologies or agendas.

Peace-building: Efforts to prevent, mitigate, or resolve conflicts by addressing the underlying causes and promoting reconciliation, dialogue, and cooperation.

Political Dissent: Expressing opposition or disagreement with established political views, policies, or authorities.

Political Disinformation: False or misleading information deliberately spread for political purposes, aiming to deceive or manipulate public opinion.

Political Extremism: The advocacy, support, or implementation of radical political ideologies, often characterized by uncompromising and extreme views.

Political Rehabilitation: Programs or interventions aimed at helping individuals disengage from extremist ideologies and reintegrate into society.

Political Violence: The use of physical force or intimidation to achieve political objectives, including acts such as riots, assassinations, or bombings.

Populism: A political approach that emphasizes the interests and needs of the common people, often by opposing the elite or established institutions.

Propaganda: Information or materials disseminated with the intent to shape public opinion, often through biased or misleading content.

Radical Discourse: Communication that employs extreme or inflammatory language to promote radical views or ideologies.

Radical Feminism: A branch of feminism that advocates for significant societal and cultural change, challenging traditional gender roles and power structures.

Radical Left: Political groups or individuals advocating for significant societal or political change through means considered outside of mainstream or centrist politics.

Radical Right: Political groups or individuals advocating for conservative or traditionalist values, often associated with strong nationalism or anti-immigration stances.

Radicalization: The process by which individuals adopt extreme political beliefs, often leading to support for or engagement in extremist activities.

Radicalization Factors: Various personal, social, economic, or political factors that contribute to an individual's susceptibility to radicalization.

Recruitment Networks: Networks or systems established by extremist organizations to identify, contact, and recruit potential members or sympathizers.

Recruitment Propaganda: Media content designed to attract individuals to join extremist groups or support their causes.

Social Media Manipulation: The deliberate use of social media platforms to spread disinformation, amplify extremist narratives, or manipulate public opinion.

Social Polarization: The widening gap and increased tensions between different social, political, or ideological groups within a society.

Symbolism: The use of specific symbols, gestures, or imagery to represent and communicate political ideologies or affiliations.

Terrorism: The use of violence or intimidation for political purposes, typically targeting civilians to provoke fear and influence policy.

Totalitarianism: A form of government that seeks to control all aspects of public and private life, imposing strict ideological conformity.

Violent Extremist Organizations (VEOs): Groups or movements that employ violence or promote extremist ideologies to achieve political, social, or religious goals.

Violent Rhetoric: Language or speech that incites or encourages violence, often directed towards individuals or groups with differing ideologies.

Xenophobia: The fear or hatred of foreigners or strangers, often manifested in discriminatory attitudes or actions.

Discussion Questions

1. What are some key factors that contribute to the rise and spread of political extremism? How can awareness of these factors help in combating extremism?

2. How can education and critical thinking play a role in countering political extremism? What strategies can be implemented in educational systems to promote critical analysis and media literacy?

3. In what ways can fostering dialogue and promoting respectful conversations across ideological divides help in combating political extremism? What are some effective methods to encourage constructive discourse?

4. How can community engagement and grassroots initiatives contribute to the prevention of radicalization and the promotion of tolerance and understanding?

5. What are some successful examples of programs or interventions aimed at countering political extremism? What are the key elements that make these initiatives effective?

6. How can social media platforms and technology companies contribute to combating extremism? What policies and measures should be implemented to address the spread of extremist content online?

7. What role can political leaders and policymakers play in combating political extremism? How can they promote inclusivity, bridge divides, and encourage moderate voices?

8. How can individuals and communities recognize and respond to extremist propaganda and recruitment efforts? What resources and support systems should be in place to assist those vulnerable to radicalization?

9. What strategies can civil society organizations, religious institutions, and NGOs employ to counter extremist ideologies and promote peacebuilding initiatives?

10. How can international cooperation and collaboration help combat political extremism? What are some successful examples of cross-border efforts in countering extremist narratives and promoting tolerance?

11. What are the ethical implications and challenges in countering political extremism? How can we strike a balance between safeguarding civil liberties and ensuring public safety?

12. How can individuals and communities promote a sense of belonging, inclusivity, and social cohesion to counter the appeal of extremist ideologies?

13. How does socioeconomic inequality contribute to political extremism, and how can addressing these disparities play a role in combating extremism?

14. What are the potential long-term effects of political extremism on democratic institutions and social cohesion? How can these effects be mitigated or reversed?

15. What role does media play in either exacerbating or mitigating political extremism? How can media organizations promote responsible journalism and counter the spread of extremist narratives?

16. How can individuals effectively engage with family members, friends, or colleagues who hold extremist views? What strategies can be employed to initiate productive conversations and bridge ideological gaps?

17. What role can religious leaders and institutions play in countering extremist interpretations of faith? How can religious teachings promote tolerance, inclusivity, and peace?

18. How can government policies strike a balance between addressing security concerns and protecting civil liberties when combating political extremism? What are the potential challenges and trade-offs?

19. How can grassroots movements and social activism contribute to countering political extremism? What examples exist of successful grassroots initiatives that have made a positive impact?

20. What are the potential consequences of stigmatizing or marginalizing individuals who hold extremist views?

How can societies effectively address these individuals while preventing further radicalization?

21. How can artistic expression, including literature, music, film, and visual arts, be utilized to challenge extremist ideologies and foster dialogue and understanding?

22. What strategies can be employed to prevent the recruitment and radicalization of vulnerable populations, such as young people or marginalized communities?

23. In what ways can international collaborations and partnerships facilitate the exchange of best practices and resources for combating political extremism? What are the potential challenges in such collaborations?

24. How can existing legal frameworks address the issue of online radicalization and the spread of extremist content? Are there any gaps in legislation that need to be addressed?

25. How can the media responsibly cover and report on political extremism without inadvertently amplifying extremist narratives or providing a platform for extremist voices?

26. How can psychological interventions, counseling, and rehabilitation programs play a role in the prevention and rehabilitation of individuals who have been radicalized?

27. How can societal values, cultural norms, and historical narratives be leveraged to counter extremist ideologies? What role does collective memory and historical education play in combating extremism?

28. How can technology be harnessed to counter political extremism? Are there innovative approaches, such as

artificial intelligence or data analytics, that can assist in identifying and addressing extremist activities?

29. How can communities build resilience against extremist ideologies? What are some successful examples of community-led initiatives that promote inclusivity, understanding, and social cohesion?

30. What role can schools and educational institutions play in fostering critical thinking, empathy, and tolerance to combat political extremism? What curricular or extracurricular activities can be implemented to achieve this?

31. How can efforts to combat political extremism balance the need for short-term security measures with the importance of addressing the underlying social, economic, and political factors that contribute to extremism?

32. What role can civil liberties and human rights protections play in countering political extremism? How can societies strike a balance between security measures and preserving fundamental rights and freedoms?

33. How can schools and educational institutions promote multiculturalism, diversity, and inclusivity to counter extremist ideologies? What approaches can be taken to ensure that education fosters tolerance and understanding?

34. How can interfaith and intercultural dialogue contribute to countering political extremism? What are some effective methods for facilitating meaningful conversations and building bridges between different religious and cultural groups?

35. How can storytelling, narrative-building, and counter-narratives be employed to challenge extremist ideologies and promote alternative, more inclusive perspectives?

36. How can psychological and social support networks help individuals who have disengaged from extremist ideologies reintegrate into society and prevent relapse?

37. How can government agencies and law enforcement collaborate with communities to prevent radicalization and detect early signs of extremist behavior without creating a climate of suspicion or eroding trust?

38. What role can economic development, poverty alleviation, and social inclusion play in countering political extremism? How can societies address underlying grievances and inequalities that may contribute to radicalization?

39. How can grassroots initiatives engage with vulnerable populations, such as disaffected youth or marginalized communities, to provide positive alternatives and pathways away from extremist ideologies?

40. How can media literacy programs and critical thinking skills be integrated into educational curricula to help individuals critically evaluate and analyze media content, reducing vulnerability to extremist propaganda?

41. What is the responsibility of online platforms and social media companies in combating political extremism? How can they effectively address the spread of extremist content and disinformation while respecting freedom of expression?

42. How can religious institutions and leaders promote interfaith dialogue and collaboration as a means of countering religious-based political extremism?

43. How can societies address the root causes of radicalization, such as grievances related to discrimination, marginalization, or exclusion, to effectively combat political extremism?

44. How can international cooperation and information sharing among intelligence agencies help prevent the cross-border spread of extremist ideologies and activities?

45. How can community-led initiatives and programs foster resilience and empower individuals and communities to reject extremist ideologies?

46. How can governments and organizations work together to rehabilitate and reintegrate individuals who have been involved in extremist activities? What are some successful models or approaches?

47. How can societies strike a balance between protecting freedom of speech and countering hate speech and incitement to violence that may fuel political extremism?

48. What role can art, culture, and creativity play in challenging extremist narratives, fostering empathy, and promoting dialogue and understanding?

49. How can early intervention and prevention programs, such as mentoring, youth engagement, and community outreach, help address the risk factors associated with radicalization?

50. What are the potential long-term strategies for combating political extremism, considering factors such as generational shifts, social changes, and evolving technological landscapes?

www.ingramcontent.com/pod-product-compliance
Lightning Source LLC
Chambersburg PA
CBHW020419290526
45785CB00002B/630